Constantinople and Byzantium

I0559619

LÉON BLOY

Translated By Richard Robinson

Sunny Lou Publishing Company
Portland, Oregon, USA
http://www.sunnyloupublishing.com

1st Edition, Revised & Corrected: January 11, 2024
Original Publication Date: July 16, 2022

ISBN: 978-1-955392-31-0

* * *

This translation from French is based on the
Éditions Georges Crès & Cie fourth edition of
Constantinople et Byzance, Paris, 1917.

Contents

Foreword

This book is a good summary of the period of Byzantium (aka Constantinople) between the middle of the 10th and the middle of the 11th centuries, with events that *lead up to* and perhaps explain, or put into context, the amazing period of the Crusades which began (First Crusade) in the very late eleventh century, with the culmination (at least for Byzantium) of the Fourth Crusade at the end of the twelfth by Europeans.

To be clear, the crusades are *not* covered at all in this book, other than mentioned several times. Merely that the events and time period covered in this book provide a good historical background for their occurrence, which started less than 50 years after the history in this book ends (in AD 1055).

Byzantium was like a wounded animal with a diamond-studded collar, around which all the animals of prey – Bulgars, Slavs, Rus (Russian), Saracens, Arabs, Venetians, Normans, etc. – circled round and took bites out of until the animal succumbed finally. It took a long while, but it ultimately succumbed. The warrior emperors – Nicephorus Phocas, John Tzimiskes, Basil II the "Bulgar Slayer" – kept the other animals at bay. But after them, not so much.

This book is different from Bloy's other historical essays or monographs – for instance, *Soul of Napoleon* – in that this one is a traditional history (a summary of Schlumberger's much more expansive history, in 3 or 4 volumes). Compared to Bloy's other histories, – which for the most part came after this one (this one was originally published in 1906, but later republished in 1917; *Soul of Napoleon* came out in 1912, and *Joan of Arc and Germany* after that), – there is very little in this book of the historical symbolism of God. Which is not to say that Bloy does not look at the events through the prism of religion, sometimes, – he does. But he keeps suchlike comments at a minimum if you will (at a minimum for Bloy).

That said, there are some really good passages in the book with interpretations and comments by Bloy that will give you shivers, – echoes of the Marchenoir passages from *The Desperate Man* novel. Historical perspectives from the p.o.v of the staunch Catholic that he was, the very particular Catholic, the French Catholic of the Belle Epoque. Enough to keep the Bloyians, such as myself, satisfied and alert – if the bloody and gruesome and decadent history contained in it was not enough.

For the one or two Bloyian scholars among us, it is interesting to note *when* the original *Constantinople and Byzantium* was written (it was originally published in 1906 under slightly different title). Unless my wires are crossed, it was *written* after he got out of Lagny, that moral sinkhole on the Marne where he subsisted from 1901-1904. He had moved out of there in 1905, and was living in Montmartre by the time, I believe, that he started writing this book.

But see *The Biography of Léon Bloy: Memories of a Friend* by René Martineau, to confirm; I believe there is mention of it there. Note, however, also that Bloy's diary from the years AD 1901-04, as contained in *Four Years of Captivity on Cochons-sur-Marne*, mentions initial contact with Schlumberger's work. He had at least ideated the work in those terrible years of his life, probably. Whether he had begun to write this book while living in Lagny is, however, to be determined.

Good American that I am, I can't help remarking that I liked some of the disparaging remarks Bloy makes about American millionaires of the time, in this work. Although the comments were made over 100 years ago, the underlying tendencies this side of the Atlantic of greed and bourgeois sentiment are much more exacerbated today, and rampant, than they were back then. Just look at the so very many but so very shallow and self-centered, not to mention self-indulgent but also decadent and really vulgar, – such as one has never seen before or imagined possible – "artists," "musicians," "actors," and media darlings, people who are famous merely for being famous, as well as some "politicians" on the national stage, etc. whom we seem in America and abroad (?) to adore, at least in the media. What would Bloy think and say today about our adorable country of America, which started out so well once upon a time, but that has since irreparably lost its way and lacks any sense of moral or ethical compass, with the only principles subscribed to now being, seemingly, those of money, self, and sex. Perhaps in that order. I tremble and then weep thinking about it. We are all, in the West, prostitutes, physical or moral, for one reason or another. I think he might have suffered a small bout of apoplexy if he learned about it or guessed at it somehow. And his faith may have, just maybe it may have, been shaken for a moment.

Is not America a little like Byzantium today – without the warrior emperors? We are being encircled by the dogs of prey more and more, and little by little, sooner than later, we will have to succumb. It is inevitable. Unless.

– RICHARD ROBINSON (in 2022, four days after Bastille Day, for all the good it did)

Dedication

To Vincent d'Indy

It is Saint Christopher who gives me the audacity to dedicate this book to you. I am assured that you love with a particular affection the admirable Giant Martyr. So marvelous an attraction, is it not a bond between you and me?

Formerly, when I was a beggar and I had to quit my job in order to transcend humiliations, I looked with confidence on the image of the Christ-Bearer, reminding myself of the old adage: *Christophorum videas, postea tutus eas*,[1] and I was fortified for suffering.

Today, having grown old and remained poor, I still and forever consult with Saint Christopher in advance of going before the Christ himself, passing through the Tenebrous Sea where I hope to have you has a companion.

Byzantium will not distract us from our path, as it is the Gate of that luminous East where the "versatile" sword of fire of the Cherubim reveal to Christian artists alone the secret of Paradise lost.

– LÉON BLOY

---

[1] *Christophorum...*: Latin for "Look on [Saint] Christopher, then go in confidence."

Preface

The Turk's domination of Constantinople, will it last through its fifth century? However decrepit it was, one hundred years ago, old Byzantium still appeared to Napoleon like "the Empire of the world." Now one would think that it was in its last agony. Asia escapes it, and the last shreds of its European territory are a vast cemetery around its walls, as at the time of the last Palaiologoses.[2]

France, Russia, England put terrible pressure on it, and the succession of the Sultans and Basileis is already almost in litigation. The old Moscovite dream of the conquest of Constantinople which revolted Napoleon will certainly not be readily accepted by the rest of Europe in arms, and it is easy to foresee, on that subject, formidable conflicts, immediately after the German Colossus' ruin.[3]

It would be desirable, for world peace, that a prodigious earthquake snuffed out forever that burning brand of concupiscence of all peoples and that an immense Propontis overran once and for all that peninsula of adversity and misfortune!

World peace! Is it to be hoped for even at such a price? I know nothing about it, and I do not believe it. The ferment is too universal and the hour when the

---

[2]Palaiologos: the eponymous and last dynasty of Byzantium (AD 1261-1453) which was founded by Michael Palaiologos VIII.

[3]German Colossus: Wilhelm II.

Holy Spirit promised to renew the face of the earth seems too near. All conjecture is impossible from here on out. No help to be hoped for from ordinary commonplaces.

The history of a multitude of centuries is before us like a poor woman who goes to die of inanition without having been able to make herself understood. The Symbolism that was her language from time immemorial will disappear with her, without any human intelligence having been able to decipher it.

The only thing possible to divine or believe is that universal history – so vainly read by Bossuet! – is a mysterious and prophetic prefiguration of God's Drama, analogous very probably to the entirety of prefigurative images that constitute Biblical Revelation, impenetrable until the High Mass of Calvary; but with this difference that the Jewish prophecy was concerned with Redemption and the universal prophecy of history is concerned with the *fulfillment* of Redemption by the triumphal advent of the Holy Spirit.

The difficulty is the same and clearly more invincible, a divine law opposing itself to intelligence *prior to* all natural or supernatural warning. It is enough to love in order to believe, but indispensable to have seen in order to understand, and from there the apparent incredulity of Saint Thomas, so strangely nicknamed the Double Abyss, is found to be justified.

We find ourselves then, today, at the edge of a precipice, deprived of faith and totally devoid of the faculty of seeing, equally incapable of loving and understanding. All that one can know of the past, for the last six thousand years, is however before our eyes: the Patriarchates, the Monarchies, the Empires, the migrations of peoples, wars, exterminations, the infinite adventures of Sorrow – to say nothing of the enormous voids, immeasurable lands of Tradition procured by cataclysms; but we have not advanced beyond it. Having never observed but the exterior and the transitory, we understand absolutely nothing about new Gestures and superhuman appearances that having nothing analogous in any past and which already seem to belong to some indiscernible Future.

If the nearest future of the whole world shies away presently from all hypotheses, from all calculations of experiment, what can one prognosticate about Constantinople? Could one cite a valid word or two on the famous question of the East, given how long a time as it has been spoken about in books or assemblies? A mysterious, irresistible force turns the heart of man towards the East which was his cradle. One has seen that in every century. Death seems to him to be situated in the sunset, and that instinct pre-existed the Crusades. No Western politics will change any of that. People will continue to bray louder and louder this side of the Light, and the time is perhaps not too far off when the vast Asian plateaus will see the frightened multitudes running to it...

Constantinople will have undoubtedly ceased to exist by then, and Theodosius or Justinian's sumptuous Byzantium, the wonder of the world, will be nothing but a memory anymore for some dreamers.

Before it disappears forever, in one manner or another, I thought it could be useful to give my testimony by showing, one last time, that famous city such as I saw it in the tenth century, when it was still the radiant and all-powerful capital of twenty prostrate nations. I offer then to those of my contemporaries who still read, a definitive re-printing of *The Byzantine Epic and Gustave Schlumberger*, published in 1906 by the *Nouvelle Revue*, a little-known and probably forgotten study.

The spectators of contemporary history will learn undoubtedly with joy the treatment inflicted on the Bulgars of that distant epoch by the redoubtable Basil nicknamed the Bulgar Slayer, who had decreed the extermination of those hereditary brigands and who had the good fortune of succeeding after twenty-five years of an atrocious war, but without being able unfortunately to extirpate their stump.

May God see to it that that desideratum of the millennial emperor be accomplished finally! Besides, Bulgaria cannot be conceived of without Constantinople. Their destinies were parallel throughout the Middle Ages and when Byzantium was trampled underfoot by the Ottomans, Bulgaria had to have had the same experience at almost the same time.

The world today is invited to an identical spectacle. The two will perish together probably, and there will no longer be any obstacles along the great Asian route that leads to the valley of Jehoshaphat.

– LÉON BLOY, Bourg-la-Reine, March 1917

Constantinople and Byzantium

The Byzantine Epic and Gustave Schlumberger

I would like someone to show me a history as discouraging as that of Byzantium. There are certainly those that are as dark, that of the nineteenth century for example. But where to find one that distresses the imagination and heart as much and that requires so much effort to shed some light on? It is twenty years already that I am slogging through books treating of the Late Roman Empire. Have I taken one step in the direction of eternal glory? That's extremely uncertain. Everything is there, however, O my religious contemporaries...

If only I had succeeded in finding the dust-covered skeleton of the Bulgar Slayer, as Michael Palaiologos' soldiers did, two hundred thirty-five years after the death of the redoubtable Basileus! They found him standing up, in the middle of ruins, that ruin of an emperor who had made a hundred million men tremble, with Melibeus' flute between his teeth. Now that is something to feed one's imagination on. But today there are no more ruins even. The historical information on one of the greatest exterminators the world has ever seen and whose reign was one of the longest, would not fill one newspaper column. The dazzling potentate's glory would not make it into the news! Yet he is merely the third of the trilogy of invincibles who, from 960 to 1025, were for sixty years the terrifying wielders of that "sword of the Dove" that Jeremiah spoke of.

He needed to be mentioned from the start, that Basil II nicknamed *Bulgaroctone* or the Bulgar Slayer, because he is, of the three, the one who takes the most space and who dug the deepest river of blood. He is, simultaneously, one of the greatest men about whom the least has been written, as if he held a secret, as if he was the formidable guardian of one of the keys to symbolic History by means of which, one day, Paradise regained is to be opened.

There had been before him, immediately before him, Nicephorus Phocas and John Tzimiskes who were, they too, extraordinary vanquishers, and I do not see a comparable suite of warrior emperors among any other people. It is what Gustave Schlumberger calls precisely the *Byzantine Epic*. Immediately after their successor Basil, one falls into an abyss. Byzantium's history becomes a horror. In vain, half a century later, Alexios Komnenos attempted to take back the sword of the Dove which had flown off into deepest heaven. It was finished, there was nothing great left except a world's interminable agony. The Fourth Crusade was the first blow of the axe on Constantinople's neck, the "City protected by God" for nine hundred years, which had a very hard life and which took two more centuries to die.

Gustave Schlumberger has just published the fourth and last volume of that Macedonian series, the most brilliant and most tragic part of the Late Roman Empire's history, from November 9, 959, date of Constantine Porphyrogenitus' death, to September 1,

1057, climactic elevation of the first Komnenos. One hundred years of a horrifyingly prodigious drama! How ever did that man, that sigillographer, that furious collector of bits and pieces of lead, dare to undertake such a task, and how is it that he was able to accomplish it in twenty years under the recoiling stars! I'm not the one who can tell you. I would have run away after the first hour. I mention it today because it is extraordinary and confounding, because the sterile academies and boring institutes cease to exist when it is a question of such great things. May it please God to give many others such a constancy of dilection!

It is dismaying to think what one needs to learn to be able to put oneself in a state of declaring with confidence that one knows nothing or almost nothing of the events that one has undertaken to recount! In the cemetery of the Grand-Montrouge there is a monument of a completely paradoxical ridiculousness, a kind of comical mausoleum, surmounted by an immensely second-rate bust, beneath which one reads stuporously the names of forty languages or dialects, followed by these words: *he knew them all!* Ridiculousness apart, Schlumberger's opus proclaims no less a panglottism. Not to mention the so-called dead languages which one cannot live without, or the many other certified living languages that contemporary imbecility mobilizes behind, he needed to assimilate idioms as cantankerous as Russian or Armenian, not to mention the grunting Saxon language which put the Comforting Angel of agonizing Jesus to flight, three hundred eighty years ago.

What to say, after that, of the archeological, numismatic, sigillographic, ethnographic and even hagiographic erudition assumed by the one hundred thirty thousand lines of meticulous documentation that makes up the four volumes of the *Byzantine Epic*? There are four volumes, in fact, in spite of the word trilogy, the author not having anticipated, when he was writing about Nicephorus Phocas twenty years earlier, that his subject would lead him along the entire length of the great Byzantine century. The heroic times end, moreover, with the death of Basil II and the thirty years that follow are the monstrously tragic tale of the most irreparable ruination ever seen since the fifth century.

The Crusades, so near at hand, would not have been possible without the enormous diminution of Byzantium. Godfrey's sword, as strong as it was, would never have been able to make a dent in the Bulgar Slayer's immense empire, from the Danube and the Adriatic to the Euphrates and the Caspian, half the Roman world under Theodosius. After the schism of the diabolical patriarch, there wasn't enough air in the East for Greeks and Latins to breathe together. When the occasion appeared right to them, the latter scaled the walls of the city that was said to be protected by God and squatted there like barbarians.

Nicephorus Phocas

The duel between Nicephorus Phocas, the Byzantine emperor, and the magnificent leader Hamdanid Sayf al-Dawla, prince of Aleppo, is one of the most heroic peripeteias of the tenth century. It is also one of the least known. And the conquest of Crete by Nicephorus, before he was emperor, – who remembers it?

And the enormous tragedy of the massacre, of the butchery of that *Cosmocrator* hacked alive by his exasperated lieutenants, who could shed any light on it? "In the black of night, on a black table, a black ant..." so goes an Eastern proverb. It is Byzantium in the tenth century. It seems that God alone might know about it and see it. The historical instruction on this point, presented by professors such as Lebeau, whom nobody reads for a hundred years now, resembles the funeral oration of universitarian Prattling. It needed Schlumberger's constancy of an Apache and his sagacity of an old Mohican with his ear to the ground to be able to draw something out of the darkness. And behold the arch-centenary mosaic unearthed, washed clean with a fervor, removed from its centuries-old gangue, as it begins to resplend again.[4]

---

[4]Original footnote: Resplend again: "The end of the tenth century and the first quarter of the eleventh is really the most obscure period of the Byzantine Middle Ages... Unprecedented thing, nobody had yet undertaken to write the complete history of that vast period since the several chapters by Lebeau!... I had to restitute it nearly from all its pieces. Nothing remotely close existed." – Introduction to *The Byzantine Epic*.

The Crusades demonetized everything, that is what is meant here. When Nicephorus Phocas, inaugurating the long Byzantine epic, was proclaimed *basileus* in Caesarea of Cappadocia by the enthusiasm of his soldiers, it was only one hundred thirty-four years later that Godfrey de Bouillon, seriously ill and carried on a litter, following his army, traversed – in his vicinity – the rude countryside of Cilicia, on his way to Palestine.

Already at that time, the work of three great basileis was destroyed and their vast empire three quarters lost. The French prince was going to become the first in that lamentable series of poor kings of Jerusalem whose territory was not even the size of a small province and which did not last more than one hundred years. The Leaders of the crusade who came after him must have been recompensed even less. None of them could do anything that lasted, some even could not succeed in arriving at the Holy Sepulcher, and the greatest of all, Saint Louis, was crushed like the others against the Mussulman breast. But they effaced the celebrated Byzantine emperors and succeeded, for some time, to supplant them. They appeared incomparably more dazzling because they were *poor* for the most part, because they were hungry and thirsty for the Tomb of Jesus Christ, because they were not only terrible heroes, but *pathetic* heroes, something that had never been seen before. No one spoke anymore about, and shouldn't have spoken anymore about, it seemed, these outdated autocrats whom the Romantics, like Walter Scott, made look like idiots in their successors.

You remember that *Count Robert of Paris*, the companion of Baldwin, Tancred, and Bohemond, who audaciously sits on the throne of the emperor Alexios and who has, immediately afterwards, such dangerous adventures? The intention of that novel was primarily to depict Byzantium and the imperial family with the same exactitude and the same conscience, alas! that Louis XI and his entourage were painted in *Quentin Durward*. One reads it at sixteen or eighteen years old and comes away with the impression of a Byzantine court orchestrated like a boulevard scene, with the courtiers or the automaton-functionaries prostrated before a doddering emperor whose power is a decor that the Western knights can smash with a single blow of their iron-gloved fist. It is the ambition of contemporary Byzantines to restitute as much as they can of the marvelous City and marvelous Empire.

The conquest of the Isle of Crete was, for Nicephorus, something like that of Egypt for Bonaparte. Immediately one felt in him the master of the world. It is hard today to conceive of the importance and the difficulty of that great military feat. Voluptuous meridional Italy, the gentle themes of Calabria and Lombardy, the Peloponnese and Thessaly of the gods, the Archipelago with its scented islands as far as the provinces closest to the heart, Macedonia and Thrace, had become, by will of black Hagarene demons, the extensions or dependencies of hell.

> *Crete, the ancient island with a hun-*
> *dred cities, which its position, half-*

way between Christian Europe and Muslim Africa, gave so great an importance to; Crete definitively lost to Europe at the same time as Sicily and Dalmatia, under the reign of the odious brute who called himself Michael II, had become the Greeks' most horrible scourge. For more than one hundred thirty years, the Arabs and their robber emirs set themselves up there, to the despair of all the populations of the Archipelagic isles and the Greek and Asiatic coasts, – incessantly ravaged by them. Chandax, modern Candia, was anymore merely the immense capital of Saracen pirates from all over the Mediterranean, a gigantic cavern of thieves that all the treasures of the East flowed into, the market where all the purveyors of harems for the Muslim world came to stock up on Christian slaves. Continually reinforced by adventurers from all the cities of Islam, the Arabs of Crete, in that impregnable place, an advanced sentinel that the Saracen lands to the south formed a kind of protective belt around, were, without great personal danger, the most terrible enemies of the Empire. Each spring, like a monstrous machine of war, Crete vomited its fleets, its innumerable and light

vessels with black sails, of marvelous
speed, which went everywhere, burning cities, razing terrified populations,
disappearing with the spoils and people of an entire city, before the imperial troops, who were always over-
worked, could run to their aid.

One needs to read, in the chronicles of
the ninth and tenth centuries, the
ghastly account of those adventures,
which were constantly reproduced in
terrifying monotony. Several hours
were often enough for those admirable
corsairs, of an agility, audacity, and
incomparable precision, to transform
a flourishing Byzantine city into a
smoking solitude. In vain, detachments
of the imperial fleet sailed constantly
throughout the Archipelago, the Dode-
canese, or Region of Twelve Islands,
as the Byzantines called it; they always arrived too late and could only
make note of a new and irremediable
disaster. The city was deserted and
burnt; the enemy had disappeared; the
sea was empty of sails; but, several
days later, the Chandax bazaars were
teeming with an immense booty, its
port could not contain the Saracen
feluccas, the African barques encum-
bered with the merchants of men from
Syria or Egypt, and in the big square,

behind the walls, interminable rows of
captives, young men, young women,
children of every age, – for everyone
that was old and useless had been
killed beforehand, – waited naked,
stunned by the despair and horrible
suffering of being piled together for a
long period of time on filthy ships,
where their new masters divvied them
up in order to lead them from there to
the edges of the Muslim world, to the
banks of Basra as well as to the
cataracts of the Nile, into the burning
solitudes of Hejaz as well as onto the
distant Andalusian shores...

There is not in all of history a more moving
episode than the taking and the sack of Thessalonica,
in 904, by the renegade Leo of Tripoli who left behind, on the onyx of the Middle Ages, a "stone of
shadows and insomnia," *lapidem caliginis et umbram*
mortis, a wake of terror that a thousand years have
not erased. In several hours, the famous city, eternal-
ized by Saint Paul, the first city of the Empire after
Constantinople, became a burning charnel house. The
Tripolitan led away twenty-two thousand young people of both sexes doomed to the most frightening
servitude – treatment reserved, I want to hope, for the
masses of delicious Christians whom the *Charity*
Bazaar has not sufficiently enlightened. That
adorable Tripolitan scoundrel possesses an apocalyptic ragout. John Kaminiates' narration is of a torturing
precision. That young priest, who had become a cap-

tive with several of his family and miraculously survived, described that massacre just as, five centuries later, Nicetas was to wail the enormous butchery of Constantinople, but with a naïvety unfamiliar to the rhetor of the time of Murtzuphlus and Baldwin.

That cannot be endured. The empire was in despair. All the same, they needed to wait for another fifty-six years! Eternity alone will make known what God's creatures had to put up with.

Many great expeditions had failed miserably. Crete was the apple of the Mussulman's eye, the least threat to it brought countless defenders running to it immediately from all the African shores. It took as much genius as boldness to attempt it, and exceptionally good luck to succeed. Already known for important successes along the Saracen frontier of Asia Minor, Nicephorus embodied, in his time, the type of the perfect warrior. By Constantine VII, he was appointed *magister*, one of the Empire's highest dignities, a "most splendid" dignity, and the great domestic of the Eastern *scholes*, that is to say the generalissimo of the Empire's forces in Asia, – the only thing he didn't possess was the crown. After his admirable victory, followed by a public triumph in Constantinople, everyone envisioned it on his head. It was really something else altogether after the stunning campaign in Cilicia and the taking of the celebrated capital of the Hamdanids, the richest and until then the most unapproachable city of Aleppo. It was, after three and a half centuries, the recommencement of Roman domination in Syria.

It was a matter for Nicephorus, the great captain and the fervent Byzantine devotee, of putting the pieces back together, at Islam's expense, of that old Roman empire, which every good son of Constantinople each day wept the fall of. What he had done for Crete, he wanted today to do for those rich provinces of Cilicia, Syria, Mesopotamia, fallen for so long a time into the hands of the sectarians of Muhammad. That man of proud, active, persevering patriotism was constantly dreaming of a restoration of ancient Roman power.

The adorable beauty of Providence demanded that that terrible soldier encounter, in order to overcome him, the living obstacle of one of the finest warriors of Islam. Sayf al-Dawla, vanquished by Nicephorus, had no end to prosperity, chivalry, magnificence. His story is like a dream, and his sad end is almost unbelievable.

For him who combs through the Byzantine chronicles of the middle of the tenth century, for more than twenty years, from 945 to 967, a unique name crops up on each page – that of the constant and indefatigable, but also most fearsome enemy of the Greek Empire. It is the name of the Prince of Aleppo, Sayf al-Dawla, the Hamdanid.

He was the perfect example of the Saracen emir of the Middle Ages, cruel, luxurious, passionately enamored with power, procuring for himself by every means immense sums of money which he had continual need for in order to pay his mercenaries, but bold, of the most brilliant, most temerarious bravery, fearless as well as lacking in weakness, chivalrous, polished, capable of the most noble and generous acts, enlightened and passionate protector of letters and arts, equally fit to inhabit the palace in A Thousand and One Nights *or a thieving Bedouin's tent. A contemporary of his depicts him as more handsome than all the children of Hamdan, whose beauty was famous: "the pearl in the middle of the necklace that they formed," eloquent, liberal. "His royal residence was an attraction for visitors, the favorite stop of voyagers, the hope of the needy, the combat arena of poets and men of letters. Never, except at the door of the Caliphs, did one see reunited around one single prince so many masters ès poetry." His court shined with the most brilliant light as long as he lived. His gorgeous suburban palace in Aleppo, El Halebah, where he loved to repose during the rare and short periods of calm which followed his incessant taking up of arms, was the universal rendezvous of men of letters, artists, brilliant representatives of that Arab society, then still so brilliant. That free son of the desert, that intrepid emir who laughed in the face of danger, that admirable and peerless knight who, accompanied by his famous body guards, spent his life in the saddle, traveling enormous distances on his courser in one day, over all the routes of Asia, who had never passed a single day without mounting the marvelous horses of his stud farm, that perfect Saracen warrior who, since early adolescence, had, each year, led into Christian lands or against his own co-religionists some stunning expedition, some devastating raid, that sumptuous sovereign who gave audience to foreign ambassadors in the décor of a dazzling, fantastic wealth, who lived in the midst of a dreamlike luxury, took pleasure stimulating the poetic ardor of his court's minstrels. In the evening, in the vicinity of his superb harem, in the embalmed gardens, alongside the cold waters of the Kouek River, in the marble-tiled courts, to the argentine sound of jets of water spreading fresh-*

*ness in the air, or even in the desert,
under his vast and sumptuous war tent
"with pillars as tall as ship masts," he
loved to listen to his favorite perform-
ers, who put his victories to verse. He
himself was a poet... Thousands of poems have been composed in his honor.
When he was pleased by them, he paid
them enormous sums for them... He
had had struck large pieces of gold
weighing ten standard dinars, espe-
cially for like recompenses.*

*The most famous of all the men of let-
ters who lived at the court of the
prince of Aleppo was the famous
Motenabbi. That man, one of the most
illustrious among so many poets of Islam, never quit Sayf's side. He lived
next to him for nearly ten years, from
948 to 957, showered with attention,
honors, and riches. "His verse," said
his Arab biographer, "spread to the
most distant cities of Arabia; they recited it at night, and piously kept memory of it during the day."*

*Nothing is harmonious, nothing ex-
hales the manly poetry of fights in the
desert and in the Syrian mountains
like Motenabbi's verse recounting the
prowess of his dear emir: "O Sayf!
You have covered all the hills with the*

*cadavers of your enemies like some-
one scattering silver coins over the
head of a new bride." Led by Sayf in
person, the knights of Aleppo swept
down onto the enemy in the middle of
a dust storm, with a forest of lances.
Their horses have a haggard look; the
dried sweat forms a brilliant covering
around their girth; one could call it a
silver belt that wraps their flanks. Sayf
surprised the women of his enemies
when they were escaping in their lit-
ters, and the blood that the feet of his
horses kicked up, splattered the breast
of the noblest of ladies. All those solitudes, surprised to see themselves visited by humans, were filled with those
fugitive women, adorned with gold
jewelry, carried by the most expensive
camels. "Your horses, o Sayf, do not
know how to eat the barley that serves
them for nutrition except when the sac
that contains it is placed on a cadaver."*

*... What curious details, full of life!
Listen again to this proud song of triumph for an Arab chief allied with the
Hamdanids: "I am the son of battles
and liberality, the son of the sword
and of the lance. Deserts and rhymed
verse, the saddles of camels and the
mountains are like a father and ances-*

*tors to me. I wear a long baldric; I live
in a tent held up by long pieces of
wood; long also is my lance and no
less long is the iron that reinforces it.
My sword precedes the death that pursues mortals; one would say that it
and death are a pair."*

All that was too beautiful for the children of
the dusty prophet. The handsome emir, already old,
fell into extreme humiliation, betrayed by his favorite
lieutenant, abandoned even by his poet, his soldiers,
and his territory, infirm and seeing, with death in his
heart, Greek bands burn his cities, expiring finally at
fifty-two years old, in despair.

*They placed, heroic detail that paints
a good picture of those ardent lords of
the tent, under the head of the cadaver
in his litter, a brick made of the pow-
der and sweat that, after each battle
against Christians, before his evening
bath, the masseur's strigil had made
fall from the skin of Sayf al-Dawla. He
himself had assiduously ensured that
that bizarre harvest was collected, his
entire life. He wanted to sleep the eternal sleep on that pillow.*

And that was the end of poetic Islam, the crescent of Muhammad was no longer to bathe its reflec-
tion in the limid waters of voluptuous parks where
poets and nightingales sang for so long a time on per-
fumed nights. The penitential and lamenting Crusades

were not too far off. Shouldn't the splendid infidels of Northern Syria have been replaced by the Egyptian or Saljuqid riffraff, whom the rude warriors of the West were preparing to fight?

The only great prince in Europe, at the advent of Nicephorus, was Otto I, second emperor of the House of Saxony, after the Fowler. His great victory at the Battle of Lechfeld, where it is said that the Hungarians lost 100,000 men, had saved Europe. He had just restored, somehow, the Empire of the West, having had himself crowned in Rome. From the time of his reign recommenced that sort of political equilibrium instituted earlier by Charlemagne and almost immediately thereafter lost again. Quedlinburg made a counterbalance to Constantinople.

The rest of the Western world is sad and somber. Certain popes and anti-popes of that time are enough to make the cornerstones sob. In France, the Carolingian dynasty is an unfortunate big tree in the process of dying. The Archangel Saint Michael, protector of the realm, is reduced to giving a nod to Hugh Capet. Other monarchies do not even exist yet for the hope or despair of men. One has difficulty imagining a period when there was not, properly speaking, France or Spain or England, or Austria, or Russia, or Prussia, or even Germany, unless in a chaotic and embryonic state.

All those future powers, insufficiently blessed by God or not yet aggregated by demons, were bawling in multitudes, on each other's shoulder, unable to assemble and identify with each other as a people.

In reality, there was only the Greek Empire that had national viscera and a head: *Autocrator* of the Romans, *Cosmocrator, Isapostole*, in other words the equal of the apostles, successor of the very pious Constantine, representing divine power on earth, etc. The divine right to reign, to massacre, and to live it up existed there only.

The throne was so sacred that it was enough merely to seize it, by no matter what execrable means, in order to become immediately intangible like the sacrament of the altar. A happy rebel, an improvised basileus, a very common thing, incarnated all of a sudden, by that alone, a kind of meat to sacrifice, and it took the utmost effort of his clemency to have only the eyes gouged out of the next rebel to the throne. One needs to read in our old Lebeau, universitarian and traditional historian, who oozes, through every pore, respect for visible authority, with what regular promptitude the most remarkable riffraff became august.

The prejudice of excessive Byzantine caducity mentioned earlier is singularly demolished, if only from a military point of view, by the very curious dissertation by Schlumberger with respect to a tactical treatise on the *Military Evolutions* attributed to Nicephorus and which would have interested Napoleon.

> *I took pleasure, he said, reading those twenty-five chapters of military art. It is the complete program of frontier warfare in the tenth century. Every-*

thing that the most accomplished Byzantine stratigos *ought to do at the head of his contingents to oppose the invasion of a Saracen force, to paralyze its march, or extract from its depredations a stunning vengeance, is minutely laid out, as if in an operation's manual for our officers enrolled in the School of war. Every case is rigorously provided for. For each malady the remedy is indicated. When I had finished the reading of those pages written in a barbarous Greek, but vibrating with a singular patriotic ardor, with a deep love for the things of national defense, with a veritable martial passion, I thought I saw pass before my eyes all those combats so greatly forgotten for so long a time, but bold, savage, incessantly intermixed with ambushes, surprises, prodigious cavalcades and which, during that secular battle of the Crescent and the Cross, have, thousands of times, bloodied the somber brushwood, the bitter defiles, the green slopes of old Mt. Taurus. I thought I heard in a dream the hurried gallop of Saracen mares carrying, through the night, across wide pasturages, their silent knights, lance and buckler lying across the pommel of their saddle, de-*

vouring space in order to swoop down upon, at the break of dawn, the Greek village, asleep and defenseless, almost holding their breath in order to escape the incessant surveillance of the trapezites, *those admirable Byzantine scouts. I dreamt of those incomparable scouts of Greek armies, veritable Uhlans of the Year One Thousand, accomplished artists in that sort of war that is unique in the world, the war of ruse against ruse, of secret ardent pursuit, of stratagems discovered one after the other, but one after the other renewed, of stunning surprises, of arm-to-arm combats. I dreamt of them, cuirass or coat of mail hidden under the thick surcoat, leading at a gallop with a surety, with a marvelous precision, that same company of audacious observations, of bold reconnaissances, which the German riders of the war of 1870 are the most formidable modern representatives of.*

Yes, they truly are the worthy predecessors of those Uhlans who have remained with us like the lugubrious personification of invasion, those indefatigable Byzantine trapezites, whose dangerous service was described in minute detail by the compiler of Nicephorus Phocas' tactic.

They are the same immensely long and rapid rides in pairs, deep behind enemy lines, in pursuit of some precious bit of information; it is the same contempt for danger, the same tranquil audacity, the same unique, unwavering resolution to be able, on return, at whatever cost, to provide precise details to the leader who placed his confidence in them, to be able to tell him all that needs to be known, the number of enemy troops, the name of the officer that commands them, in which direction they are preparing to go, the probable goal they have laid out for themselves; there are, in order to succeed at procuring that information, the same ingenious efforts, the same display of multiple ruses, the same perfection of all procedures of information-gathering, the same inventive genius, the same discipline assisted by the same code of punctual, precise instructions, without gaps, coupled with that immense difficulty moreover of all the insufficiencies of that relatively barbarous epoch. They are seriously mistaken, those who willingly believe that the Eastern wars of that epoch consisted merely in a succession of confused melees, of disordered collisions between savage hordes. The

> *basileis' domestics, the Hamdanid*
> *emirs (for the Saracens followed as se-*
> *vere a tactic, obeyed as rigorous a dis-*
> *cipline [as the Byzantines did]) waged*
> *war knowledgeably; they commanded*
> *highly organized regular armies. Ev-*
> *erything was laid down in advance,*
> *regulated, down to the daily service of*
> *each squad of scouts, down to that of*
> *each isolated courier.[5]*

And now, if one thinks on the *absoluteness* of that already thrice secular quarrel between Christians and Muslims, which showed no signs of abating, five hundred years later, except with the irreparable fall of Constantinople; if one considers that that was a veritable duel to the death, the longest, the most furious, the most implacable that has ever been, one will have little difficulty conceiving what had to be, by like means, the atrocity of the episodes. The taking of Anazarbus in Cilicia and, some months later, that of Aleppo, even before the victor of Crete became em-

---

[5]Original footnote: Having [the need] to demolish one of the stupidest of historical commonplaces, I thought it necessary to cite the entire passage. But a reservation is in order. Having fought in 1870, in a body of scouts to be precise, having been a well-placed witness by consequence to the indiscipline and ignoble cowardice of the Uhlans, bold against women only, and whom any resolute man could put to flight when they were a little less than twelve to one, I have the duty and the need energetically to reprove Schlumberger's admiring expressions. It may be that some one or another of those adventurers full of sauerkraut was truly intrepid, here and there. But, in general, what a bunch of cowards! What a loathsome lot of scoundrels! as the Spanish partisans said, with less reason, about Napoleon, in 1808.

peror, had that character of pure inexorableness, among so many others, which makes history slip through one's fingers and a person ask, while sobbing, why the Son of God came to die on earth.

> *In the early dawn, on Tuesday, December 23, 962, the day before the vigil of the Holy Feast of the Nativity of our Lord, the great city of Aleppo fell back into the hands of Christian soldiers, after having belonged for more than three centuries to the Saracens. It was a colossal butchery, one of those appalling scenes of universal butchery, which the East's terrifying history has seen some frightening example of each year. Real rivers of blood flowed through the narrow lanes, vaulted for the most part as some are still today. 100,000 soldiers battered, sabered, and violated a population of people struck with panic, thinking of nothing else than how to escape by any means. Only the fatigue of the assailants stopped the carnage, according to Aboulfaradj. They kept from slaughter no more hardly than the most beautiful women and the most beautiful children of either sex, numbering 10,000. The girls were destined to fill Byzantine gynæceums; the boys were to compose future schools of elite corps of the imperial guard. After the*

carnage came the pillage. The opulent capital of Hamdanids was totally devastated by those terrible bands from the North. The booty was so great that they could not think of carrying it all away. They had to leave the majority of it to the flames, the immense number of beasts of burden being found absolutely insufficient for that transport. The rage to destroy, so unpolitical a procedure in appearance, but which one must, I repeat, refrain from condemning straightaway, insofar as we know only very imperfectly the circumstances of those sanguinary battles, was pushed to its extreme limits. Everything was broken, devastated, annihilated. A curious example proves it. Provisions of olive oil were conserved in huge basins of masonry, veritable man-made lakes. The Byzantines made the water from nearby fountains flow into them; the oil, rising to the surface, overflowed everywhere, and the entire harvest was ruined. This detail, taken from a chronicler, speaks volumes about that pitiless and monstrous annihilation of an entire vast city.

Never before had a Byzantine army conquered by assault so important an Arab capital, and taken so much

*booty. Every chronicler is unanimous
in insisting on this fact. The boutiques
of the immense bazaar provided incal-
culable treasures. Nicephorus' battle-
hardened soldiers were amply recompensed for that long campaign that,
from the shores of the Bosphorus and
the banks of Crete, had led them as far
as the burning campaigns of the Euphrates and the Oronte. The Byzantine
foot soldiers, pursuing through the
tortuous and somber lanes, through
the labyrinth of the bazaars, the Saracen women of Aleppo, avenged uncon-
scionably three centuries of unprecedented suffering by all those unfortunate Christian populations of Asia Minor and Syria; above all, they avenged
the more recent misfortunes, those
monstrous raids that, each year, "the
impious Chamdas and his squadrons
lighter than the wind" had executed in
the land of Rum. Among the savage
natives of Cappadocia, Isauria, and
Lycaonia who composed the greatest
part of Nicephorus' foot battalions
and who, without a second thought,
slaughtered the beautiful Syrian wom-
en on the cobblestone streets of Aleppo, how many were there among them
whose wives, mothers, sisters had perished, they too, massacred in their rus-*

*tic homes beyond the Taurus moun-
tains by the fierce Hamdanid Bedouins. How many had been taken away,
bound to the back of camels in their
convoys, to suffer the agony of a loathsome captivity in the faraway harems
of the sons of Muhammad!...*

*With the massacre and the pillage
came still other excesses. A large part
of the city, all the bazaars, all the most
beautiful homes, were set on fire. The
superb mosques, decorated in faience
and admirable stuccoes, which made
the glory of Aleppo, were given the
pick of demolitioners, their deliciously
sculpted or incised* members *were
burnt and the ashes thrown to the
wind. Salt was sown into their cursed
places. Others, after having been puri-
fied, were probably made over for one
day at least to the Christian cult. The
great mosque, "one of the marvels of
the world," to listen to the Mussulman
chroniclers, similar to that of Damascus, and which had been constructed
at great expense by Sulayman ibn Abd
al-Malik, was pillaged, burnt, transformed into a stable for Byzantine
mares.*

Finally, let's take a look at the emperor
Nicephorus, after several adventures. He wed the

stunning, diabolical Theophano, widow and probable poisoner of Romanos II, his predecessor. Schlumberger frees her of any guilt for that crime, and I'm terribly upset about it. It would have been much nicer. Romanos II, miserably cut down at twenty-two years old, was not wept for by anyone. That ignoble basileus lived only for his belly and the appendices of his belly, to borrow Leon Diacre's expression, annoyingly attenuated by Schlumberger.

However the marriage of the new master to the august vagabond was not without its difficulties. A question of "spiritual affinity," infinitely serious thing in Byzantium, intervened and an enraged patriarch's obstinacy nearly forbade everything. The Schism between the East and West capitals of the Church not due to come to a head for another hundred years, Nicephorus could have had recourse to the Pope, whom the canons of the Greek Church would not have intimidated. But he himself was too Greek and perhaps also too *Cretan* after his conquest not to prefer deceit to that arbitrage. Whatever the case, he had to follow his destiny which could not fail to be extremely tragic, above all with such a consort.

There was a high price to pay, however, for being empress and that was a tough profession being *autocratorissa*. In our days of the automobile and aerial bombs, one is not aware that ceremonies in Byzantium lasted entire days.

> *Theophano, seated, very erect, very immobile, on her high golden throne, at the back of the large hall of recep-*

*tion in the gynæceum, surrounded by
her protospathaire eunuchs, her face
painted in bright colors, her body
wrapped in her long golden loros, like
a narrow sheath, which had just replaced her mourning costume, her
shoulders draped in the heavy, multi-
color coat with large diamond shapes
brocaded in pearls and rubies, looked
like some strange and flamboyant an-
tique idol disappearing beneath the
silk, precious stones, and metal. On
her head, the diadem, with a triple
row of pearls, gleamed. Her hand held
a branch, the masterwork of Byzantine
goldsmithery. She watched, humbly
bent before her, all the palace eunuchs
pass before her, "all those who were
beardless," the only men admitted into
her presence. When she had had
enough of those pallid and important
individuals, the long procession of
women began. The prepositor, leader
of the eunuchs, assisted by the porters,
introduced according to the rites before the August queen, by successive
groups or vela, following an im-
mutable hierarchical order, the spous-
es of all the dignitaries holding rank
at court, each wife designated by her
lord's title or function. The most important by rank, in other words the*

*zōstē patricians who were always al-
lowed entrance into the Palace, presented themselves first, supported on
either side by two silentiary eunuchs,
each kneeling difficultly in sumptuous
attire so as to kiss the knees of the un-
moving Basilissa, officially indifferent,
abstaining by etiquette to lower her
eyes on whomsoever it might be, as if
lost in a haughty dream, not seeming
even to perceive the immense cortege
that defiled at her feet. After the zōstē
patricians, wives of magistrates and
patricians, came the protospatharissæ
and the spatharissæ, wives of so many
military dignitaries, followed by the
hypatissæ, the stratorissæ, the comitis-
sæ, the candidates, the wives of scri-
bones, domestics, silentiaries, man-
dataries, and a whole host of other officers of the navy or army, one hundred other classes still, brilliant fe-
male battalions disappearing into and
winding their way through the maze of
the gynæceum...*

*The triumphant beauty of that creature
infused an extreme charm into the too
rare ceremonies wherein the inflexible
rigorism of etiquette permitted her to
show herself aloof from the crowd, immobile and adorned to the extreme,
next to the little basileis, her sons. She*

appeared then like a sort of mysterious divinity, supported by her ladies in waiting and her eunuchs, without whom she couldn't have moved. Truly like a beautiful icon that had climbed out of and down from its frame, in spite of her already bad reputation, she seemed, in the eyes of the naïve pleb, the very incarnation of Theotokos,[6] queen of heaven, mother of all Byzantines. And Nicephorus contemplated her with love, little imagining the terrible future that so foolish a union would, one day, secure for him."

I cannot keep myself from experiencing a very lively feeling for that low woman of sovereign beauty, of base extraction, and profoundly vicious.

Leon Diacre, a contemporary, called her the most beautiful, most seductive, most refined woman of her time. That great sinner, whose charms must have exerted so fatal an influence, which would cause her to be loved by three emperors in succession and to be the mother of two more, was born probably in Constantinople itself, in her father's shop, the cabaret owner named

---

[6] *Theotokos*: Greek for "Bearer of God," viz., the Mother of God. Apparently a common designation for the Virgin Mary in the Orthodox Catholic Church.

Craterus. Her real name was Anasta-
so, a bar maid or servant's name. She
changed it early in life to that of the
more elegant Theophano. Leon Diacre
tells us that she was originally from
Laconia, perhaps Lacedaemonia even,
precisely finally from that Pelopon-
nesian theme, whose inhabitants the
Porphyrogenitus betrays so mediocre
a liking for in his writings. The entire
first part of Theophano's life is un-
known to us. We do not know how the
ravishing daughter of a poor, Laconi-
an cabaretier made such rapid pro-
gress in the paternal boutique of the
imperial gynæceum. We do not know
either how the said Constantine Por-
phyrogenitus was compelled to give
his consent to so undesirable a
union... Undoubtedly, the gorgeous
plebeian woman must have made the
young Romanos madly in love, and the
weak Basileus, who adored his son,
could not resist his fulgerating adoles-
cent supplications...

One understands that the chaste vanquisher of
Islam damned himself in turn for that succubus.

Nicephorus' triumphant expedition and definitive conquest of Cilicia, in 965, was perhaps Byzantium's greatest military effort. The imperial army, according to Leon Diacre, according to Arab historians

as well, numbered no less than 400,000 combatants. As apocalyptic as that of Jerusalem were the sieges of Mopsuestia and Tarsus, natal city of St. Paul, enormous cities, the teeming entrails of the immense Muslim world. They could not kill everything, the life of an executioner is too short, but once the cities were taken, they chased hundreds of thousands of captives before them, who perished for hunger in the horrible devastating campaigns.

> *Tarsus, reconquered, was immediately purified of the filth of the infamous cult of Muhammad. However, there was no destruction, and Nicephorus demonstrated a certain moderation. Only, the great mosque's enclosure was transformed into a gigantic stable for the Byzantine cavalry. That was, ordinarily, the first reciprocal affront that the Greeks and the Saracens made after the taking of a city. For three centuries, thousands upon thousands of Christian churches had echoed with the footfalls of Arabian mares, and the raucous cries of the savage grooms from the desert had many a time replaced, under profaned vaults, the pious chanting of orthodox priests. The emirs' horses had eaten their oats from the altar of all the basilicas in Syria, and the sacred vessels had served to quench their thirst. Haggard dervishes had everywhere*

rigged themselves out with sacerdotal vestments, and the bishops' crosses and processional crosses served as their walking sticks. Christians treated their hereditary enemies in the same way. According to custom, those two palpable symbols of the Prophet's religious domination: the pulpit, a gorgeous piece of sycamore wood, entirely inlaid with mother-of-pearl and delicately sculpted, and the no less rich tribune, the Khutbah, from which, since the conquest of Tarsus, public prayer had been recited every day in the name of the Caliph, – they were to be solemnly burned in the presence of the Basileus, and their cursed ashes thrown to the wind.[7]

The redoubtable Nikfour, as he was referred to by Arab writers, could have shown himself more severe, having to avenge the enormous, recent disaster of one of his armies in Sicily, from which the Greeks were evicted forever.

---

[7]Original footnote: ... to the wind: At the risk of going off topic seemingly, why wouldn't I point out, like a touching and profound thing, Gustave Schlumberger's love for the most humble vestiges of Byzantine history, his caresses for a small, poor piece of money, unique witness to the siege of Tarsus, a silver dirhem struck in Tarsus itself, in the name of Sayf al-Dawla, in the year 354 of the Hegira, the same year that Nicephorus' army seized the city (v. *Un Empereur byzantin*, p. 491); Schlumberger is a historian *in love* and that is without a doubt the greatest thing one can say.

That strange emperor appears to have had, his whole life, a nostalgia for the cloister. It is surprising when one reads that "that same man became by love for the public good, the courageous and declared adversary of religious orders and was so opposed to their incessant desires for aggrandizement that he attracted to himself, because of it, the hatred of the entire clergy."

One was easily a devotee in Byzantium. Supernaturalness was intact in the tenth century, at least as regards formulas and observances, and Nicephorus' religious zeal did not set him apart. His terrible passions of an Asiatic exasperated his fervor by throwing him into the most rigorous of practices. An old story says that the emperor's bed was fitted with shards of glass. He was hacked to death on that bed, one winter night, when he was fifty-seven years old.

Ever since Earthly Paradise was lost, the ascetic life has always been the most burning human desire. What are the rages of cupidity or ambition compared to that fire of a soul that wants to repatriate with God, to find in itself the forests and the clearings of primordial Innocence, with birds of delights and amorous ferocious beasts, when the Disobedience of man had not yet covered their eyes in blood.

> *"...They were full of fervor and ardently sighed for God," said the admirable visionary Anne-Catherine Emmerich, speaking of the holy men who lived in the ages before Jesus Christ. "I saw them often, during the*

day or during the night even, running
in solitude while invoking God and
crying to him with so violent a desire
that they tore their habits in order to
unbare their breasts, as if God should
have penetrated their hearts with the
burning rays of the sun, or as if, by the
light of the moon and stars, he should
have quenched the ardent thirst they
had for the accomplishment of the
Promise."

After Calvary, the Easterners, by whom the
faith was delegated to us, had put that into the eyes
and into the hearts of the Westerners, who imitated it
as best they could. But the most superhuman houses
of Saint Benedict or Saint Bruno were no match for
the angelic groups of the Thebaid or Syria. In the
tenth century, the times of Anthony, Pachomius, Hi-
larion were long gone. The ancient Faith which had
watched over – like a pastor of little goats – the
bounding hills, seemed outdated. Without a doubt, the
lamentable schism was not consummated. Another
three or four generations were needed. Eastern Christianity had become Greek and even *orthodox*, alas!
just as one still sees it today. The torch of love had
passed into other hands, and when the poor knights of
France came before the sun to liberate Jesus Christ's
tomb, the degenerate children of the early martyrs and
first solitaries were greater enemies to them than the
Turks or the Saracens. One guesses at what the
monastic spirit could have become.

Among the six of Nicephorus' Novellae or constitutions that have survived, there is one that shows how far, even in ecclesiastical matter, – a redoubtable pitfall for those tenth-century souls of such strict piety, – how far I say Nicephorus carried his qualities of intelligent moderation, of very broad liberalism for that time period.

That extremely devout man who had so cherished and so often listened to Saint Athanasius,[8] who loved to surround himself almost uniquely with religious, who wore a cilice, who had put onto his coins the effigies of Christ and Theotokos, who, after the conquest of Crete, had put aside, from his personal share of the booty, the enormous sum of one hundred pounds of gold as a contribution to the founding of the Laura monastery on Mount Athos, the greatest and richest convent on the holy mountain, where he had planned to retire definitively, who had given to it as well the great bronze doors for its narthex, that emperor, because of his great military preoccupations, his constant concern to assure the regular recruitment of imperial armies, had had enough independence

[8]Saint Athanasius: Athanasius the Athonite (AD 920-1003).

of mind to be very seriously anxious about the ever-growing number of monks and to seek a remedy for that grave abuse.

That large wound of the orthodox Church: the miserable caloyer, of coarse ignorance, absolutely useless, pullulated in the empire during the tenth century. One could not take one hundred steps in the streets of a Byzantine city, whether that was the capital of the least forgotten burg of Cappadocia or the Peloponnese, without bumping into one of those sordid, ragged religious, in their short and coarse vestment, with the unkempt beard, who, barefoot, muttered some unintelligible prayer, while exploiting the pious credulity of the faithful. Not a village that did not have, at the very least, its small or large monastery. Not a city that did not contain several. Everywhere, on the infinite plains as on the mountain tops, on all the slopes as in all the valleys, on the islands as well as on the solitary shores of all those endless coasts of the immense Empire, thousands of cellules of cenobites had beed erected. The ardent desire, in those exceptionally difficult times, to carve out for oneself, by religious habit, a somewhat peaceful fu-

ture, a somewhat sheltered life, the need, which was very natural in those days of violence and interminable devastations, to huddle together and thus carry out an existence more exempt from peril; the perspective primarily of escaping military service, that terrible servitude of the Empire's populations, had prodigiously developed, after many long years already, that vast monastic family. In Constantinople itself and in its faubourgs, the monasteries numbered in the hundreds. Not one church, not one chapel that did not have its own. Not an emperor, not a prince of the blood, who had not founded and magnificently endowed many. In certain quarters, the convents and pious foundations of all sorts succeeded one another in a row, across interminable distances. Many contained an enormous population. The single convent of Stoudios, that monastery dedicated to the Precursor, was inhabited by a thousand monks. What to say about the large agglomerations of Athos, the large lauras of the Peloponnese, where veritable armies of religious lived? Mount Olympus literally teemed with solitaries. In that epoch of incessant warfare which decimated generations of men just come of age, one conceives what danger and what loss for the Empire that world of monks represented, monks who numbered in the hundreds of thousands, who deprived the army of so many vigorous arms, who, in many circumstances, could become a very fearful element of fanatic agitation. And yet, the devout mind of the century, joined to enumerated causes, constantly contributed to enlarge in almost infinite proportions that already so great peril. Every opulent senator, every provincial archon or enriched shopkeeper, every woman of quality founded or enriched, during one's life or on one's deathbed, some monastery in order to attract divine clemency or redeem some very grave fault.

Little by little the national riches passed into the hands of the congregations, just as in France under the ancien regime. *The Empire threatened to become the property of a million religious.*

Nicephorus did not dream of dispossessing them, which was doubtless impossible, but he formally interdicted the establishment of new monasteries or new pious foundations and wanted to send into the desert, conformant with the spirit of their institution, the majority of monks who populated the cities. His account of motives is very curious for the epoch.

> *"The monks, he said, "do not possess any of the evangelical virtues; at every minute of their existence, they think only of acquiring new possessions of land, one arpent after the other, of building immense constructions, of buying, in innumerable quantities, horses, cattle, camels, all sorts of beasts of burden; they consecrate in that way all their force, all their energy in order to enrich themselves, such that the life they lead in reality is no different than that of the most worldly people. That totally frivolous existence – what a contrast it offers," the pious imperial jurist exclaimed, "to the life of religious saints who, in past centuries, lived in Egypt and Palestine, those whose quasi immaterial existence was more like that of the angels than that of men!"*

That famous constitution was unfortunately abrogated forty years later. He was not forgiven for it, but what brought the exasperation to a head was his pretension to nominate the bishops himself, a rather imbecilic exasperation given the so-called Orthodox Church's being already separate in fact from the Vicar of Jesus Christ; the episcopacy could no longer be conferred except by the Patriarch who was himself, nine times out of ten, a creature of the Emperor.

Nothing, to tell the truth, was forgiven him, that superior but antipathetic man, and, from the start of his glorious reign, universal discontentment began to grow, which was bound to drag him to his slaughter.

The poor wretch got to the point of steeling himself against his people. The Palace of Boukoleon, formerly built by Theodosius, was transformed on his orders into a formidable donjon, "a supreme refuge in case of sedition, the fortress intended to keep that turbulent plebs of the capital in check." Those works were a new occasion for enormous expenses, pitiless corvées. Nicephorus, always pressed for money in order to support his all-consuming armies, and unscrupulous for the most part in the means of procurement, already had a terrible reputation for greed. It was the last straw. There was nothing but angry cries in Constantinople.

> *What's more, Nicephorus was really unlucky. All his preparations, that Palace of Boukoleon, that symbol of slavery, "that acropolis constructed so as to better oppress the unfortunate citizens of Byzantium," the enormous expenses occasioned by those gigantic works, kept extraordinarily popular animosity alive, ably exploited by the ever more numerous adversaries of the present regime. People no longer went out of their way to hide criticizing the emperor, almost before his very eyes, at the Palace. As always,*

the imbecilic people gave credence to the most absurd storytellers. Nicephorus, it was said, would never have decided to wall himself in with crenelations if it weren't for an evil prophecy that had frightened him. A monk, according to some, an astrologist, according to others, had predicted to him that he would not perish except by the hand of an inhabitant of Constantinople... One night, when the famous wall was still under construction, a mysterious voice that seemed to come from the waves of the Sea of Marmara cried out, "O Basileus, it is in vain that you are having these high ramparts built. You could have them built to the skies, but you would not escape the misfortune that pursues you into your domicile, and your enemies will penetrate it without any difficulty." On Nicephorus's order, the gloomy and nocturnal promenader was sought after for a long time. No one was found. "The Basileus could not escape his destiny," said the same chronicler, and the people did not fail to make the same remark that "the prince, who had proven himself unworthy of his subjects, was murdered, on the very day that the Palace of Boukoleon was completed, when the

keys to the doors had been solemnly
handed over to him."

Before we get to the terrible denouement of
that six-year tragedy which was the reign of Nicephorus, it is necessary to point out, in chapter XIII, the re-
freshing and sedative summary given by the embassy
of Luitprand, who was sent by Otto the Great to Constantinople. That poor bishop of Cremona, retained in
spite of himself and constantly scorned by the Emper-
or, who appeared to be much amused by his ridiculousness, left a detailed account of his disappoint-
ments at the Byzantine court, which account is one of
the most precious contemporary documents. It is hard
to imagine an ambassador being treated with so little
respect. During four months of the most hateful so-
journ, there was not a single humiliation or snubbing
that was not inflicted on him. Every evening, the atra-
bilious whipping boy, after having retired to the appalling living quarters that had been assigned to him,
avenged himself of his affronts by recounting them
for the most distant posterity, painting for us a picture, of the darkest and most troubling sort, of the
Basileus and his counselors.

"Nicephorus," he said, "is of a rare
ugliness, very short in stature, with a
very fat head, very small eyes, the eyes
of a mole, a short and bristling beard,
which is thick and already greying,
with a very thin neck. He is dark in
complexion like a black man, so much
so that he would cause fear in whoev-

*er might run into him at night. He has
a fat belly and narrow hips; his thighs
are too long, his calves are too short,
his feet are deformed." The grudge-
bearing prelate does not even spare
the splendid imperial ceremonial costume which he says is too worn, nor
the famous purple boots and all the
rest of it which he greatly disparages.
That very unflattering portrait is in no
way redeemed by the depiction of
moral qualities. "The Basileus' language is insolent and brutal. He is
wily like a fox, a liar of the same cal-
iber as Ulysses... What a contrast to
you, o my noble emperor, o my dear
empress!" claims the old courtier, in
his naïve desire to please. "How much
more beautiful, more likable, more
civilized you are!"*

An important part of this relation concerns the
execrable meals, which the ambassador and his ret-
inue had to put up with. Terrible grief for those deli-
cate stomachs habituated to odoriferous wines from
Lombardy and Piedmont, forced to swallow the atrocious wine of the Greeks, an undrinkable mixture of
lime, resin, and pitch, familiar enough, in our own
days, to those who have spent even a small amount of
time in Hellenistic climes. The ambassador's prison
was even entirely lacking in water... One can imagine
for oneself how a gourmand of Cambacérès sort got
along in the presence of the abominable *garon*, the fa-

mous sauce highly appreciated by Byzantines, a kind of caviar or brine of divers types of fish, that they empoison all their dishes with and that the most intrepid or hungriest Westerners cannot envisage without horror.

Finally, after one hundred twenty days of captivity and dreadful boredoms, the discomfited negotiator for Charlemagne's heir obtained permission to leave Byzantium, and the return trip, wherein he was subject to three months of brigandage by the navigators or imperial functionaries, put a cap on the series of tragicomic tribulations undergone by that unfortunate diplomat.

In 968, the penultimate year of his reign, Nicephorus made an expedition to Asia, triumphal march across Syria and Phoenicia.

> *After having spent two months ravaging the countries situated on the two slopes of Lebanon, while the Muslim world continued fighting amongst themselves, the emperor Nicephorus, leaving a garrison in the principal fortress that he had conquered, appeared finally before Antioch, on the eighteenth day of the month of November, 968, leading after him 100,000 prisoners, almost all children or young people of both sexes. All who were old or weak had been killed or abandoned, save 1,000 old men and old women to whom Nicephorus en-*

trusted to watch over that youth. Eighteen cities with a large mosque and innumerable fortresses, secondary cities or villages, had been taken and in great part destroyed or burnt. A great number of inhabitants in Syria and along the Phoenician coast had embraced Christianity in order to save themselves.

The great Antioch, third largest city in the world, was going to be conquered by his lieutenants in its turn. In all Mussulman cities, true believers shed bitter tears. It was a merely matter of the redoubtable projects of the invincible Nikfour, who spoke of nothing short of making the name Saracen disappear from the face of the earth, as was said in the crossroads of all good towns of Islam.

"It is then even, in that abyss of distress," the old historian Aboulfeda piously exclaimed, "that God revealed himself again to afflicted Mussulmen and delivered them suddenly from a frightening torment. And that same year which had seen the triumph of the Empire by Nicephorus, who had seen him devour Syria which was completely sacrificed to his impious ambitions, who had made the entire world of the faithful children of Allah tremble at the mere mention of his name, saw that great conqueror perish in the am-

bushes of a weak woman."

Here is a passage from the Syrian historian, Yahia, who summarizes in an arresting manner those terrible campaigns by Nicephorus against the Saracens:

> *Nobody doubts that the emperor Nicephorus conquered all the Syrian provinces, the Diâr Modar, the Diâr Rabî'ah, and the Diâr Bekir, or that he has taken possession of them. In fact, he had firmly decided to invade the outlying areas of the cities and villages that he chose, to raze them, to set them on fire, to lead the inhabitants into captivity and to make off with the animals, and, with the time of the harvest having arrived, to leave, to burn all the crops and to leave thus to die of famine the inhabitants of the cities. He continued to act each year in that manner in their regards, until necessity constrained them to hand their cities over to him. He made himself master by that means of the all the frontier cities of Syria and Djezirah; he killed and reduced to captivity a number of inhabitants that God alone could count. It is at this point that his expeditions became like pleasure parties for his troops, it being understood that he committed those ravages with-*

out encountering a single Mussulman to repulse them. On multiple occasions he pursued the Bedouin Arabs and vanquished them; after those successes they were afraid of him and did not dare to approach him anymore. He inspired the greatest terror in Mussulmen. Nobody dared to stand in his presence. He submitted Bulgaria to the Russians and delegated his authority over that country. Finally, all was under his thumb and he governed with the greatest hability and the greatest success, but when he had reached the accomplishment of his desires, he was murdered.

Et post hæc decidit in lectum, et cognovit quia moreretur.[9]

Grave political concerns necessitated the hero's brusque return to Constantinople. "The reception that was made for him on his arrival, around the month of January 969, was magnificent in every way; but this time it seems as though it was an imposed enthusiasm, a simple official enthusiasm; his people's heart no longer beat in unison with his as in the fine days of his victories over Crete and his first triumphs in Cilicia. Ten years of incessant warfare, crushing military taxes enforced with the most pitiless rigor, a general food shortage occasioned less by bad harvests

---

[9]Et post...: Latin for "And after this he died in bed, and knew he was going to die."

than by the lack of hands, universal poverty, a thousand other causes of miscontent created in part by the personal and hard character of the Basileus, had rapidly transformed the former feelings of love into a deep hatred, a hatred still very little disguised in the upper class ranks, an almost open hatred in the rank and file. When the valiant warrior, the dominator of those famous Hamdanids, passed pensive, at the pace of his courser, through the streets of his immense capital which was in celebration, among all the people lined up along his passage, he must have caught sight of more than a sinister glance, heard more than a muted, discontented booing for the presence of his barbarian guards,[10] more than an scarcely dissimulated imprecation.

Nicephorus had not only become hateful to his people and to many of his companions in arm, he had become hateful also to his wife, the empress Theophano. The beautiful but corrupt empress must have grown tired for a long time already of this glory hound. The great domestic Tzimiskes, a hero himself and extremely seductive, inspired in her a passionate love. She decided to put him on the throne and let him into her bed. Tzimiskes, disgraced and deeply humiliated by the suspicious emperor, seems not to have hesitated for a single minute.

Feeling instinctively that the hour had come and that the road was open to

---

[10]barbarian guards: The Varangian Guard, composed exclusively of foreigners, at various times Rus, Norsemen, Scandinavians, later Anglo-Saxons.

him, that Nicephorus had done his time, that the unpopularity of his old brother in arms, of the man whom he had greatly contributed to making emperor, had reached its limit, he found himself, as the veritable man of his century and of his race,[11] ready to try anything, resolved to recur to the last extremes in order to seize power in turn...

He had no trouble in grouping around himself several determined men who had something to complain about with respect to the Basileus. The complot went forward with precision and a frightening rapidity. On the night of December 10, 969, at a time of cold and snow and infinite sadness, the great emperor was woken up – for several minutes, – by his assassins.

After having succeeded, against all odds, in penetrating the Palace full of traitors and spies, the conspirators leaving the platform of the Kastron, entered all together, swords drawn, into the imperial cubiculum. *The Arab historian Aboulfeda affirms that Theophano led them in person and that it was she who opened the hidden door that she had neglected to lock in the evening. The fact seems unlikely. Jean Tzimiskes was still the last person to*

---

[11]Original footnote: Tzimiskes was Armenian.

*enter into the chamber of his old com-
panion in arms. When they drew near
to the bed, they found it empty! Igno-
rant of Nicephorus's habits, they
thought they had been betrayed. Understanding that it would be impossible for them to escape, a dreadful panic seized them.*

*Already some of them were talking
about jumping into the sea from the
high walls and escaping by swimming.
A little eunuch, who had guided them
there helps them out. He points out
with his finger, in an angle of the
apartment, the Basileus deeply asleep
on his tiger skin. Immediately, everyone, like beasts of prey, surround him.
As he continued to sleep, they all
threw themselves at him at the same
time, kicking him. Awakened with a
start, he raises himself up on one arm.
Then Leon Balantes, with a terrible
blow of his sword, strikes his face
which was uncovered, his bonnet having fallen to the ground in his effort to
get up. Mad with pain, for the weapon
had sliced into his face, deeply cutting
his forehead, eyebrow, and eyelid, and
penetrating as far as the bone without
however reaching the brain, the poor
wretch cries out several times: "Theotokos, help me!" Blood is running*

*down his face; they bind his legs to-
gether; they drag him from the foot of
the large bed where John Tzimiskes
was seated; they want to make him
kneel before his old brother in arms,
but bound as he is, dazed by the blow
he had just received, he cannot keep
himself upright, and he falls over onto
the ground. John hurls the most furious invectives at him; all the conspirators follow suit; each one throws his
insult or his vengeance into his face.
"Answer me, you miserable 'tyrant,'"
cried the Armenian beside himself,
stamping on him, "answer me: tell me
whether it is not because of me that
you mounted the throne, that you became an all-powerful emperor. For-
getful of all my benefits, blinded by
basest envy, you made me fall into disgrace, you removed my command of
the army from me, you sent me to live
in the fields in miserable exile, with
peasants and valets, me, who am one
hundred times more worthy than you,
whom everyone loves and venerates
while everyone hates you. Now you
are in my power, nothing will remove
you from my hands. And yet, if you
have something to say in your defense,
speak, and I will listen to you."*

But the Basileus, feeling faint, feeling

at a loss, said nothing to so many out-
rages; only he continued to invoke out
loud the assistance of God and
Theotokos. They fiercely attack the un-
fortunate man, tearing off tufts of his
beard. They break his jaw; they knock
out his teeth with the pommel of their
sword. John, kicking his body which
was already inert, strikes him square
in the face with his sword, which splits
his skull. These ferocious men blinded
with hate take turns hitting him. One
avenges a long exile, the other his dis-
grace and his contempt of the master
for having taken the great Syrian
fortress.

Finally, on hearing the noise of the
Palace which begins to awaken and is
filled with menacing sounds, they un-
derstand that they must bring it to a
close. A conspirator, with his long
sword curved to a point, transpierces
Nicephorus through and through. The
Basileus expires immediately. Thus
died miserably, the great emperor
whose innumerable triumphs had
earned him the name of νικητής, the
victor. Theophano must have been be-
hind the door, listening.

However that dreadful scene lasted a
long time. Vague rumors made the

servants who had remained loyal sus-
pect some danger for their master.
They run to the spot. Soldiers,
Varangians perhaps, who are, that
night, on guard at the sacred Palace,
rush forward, ax in hand in the hope
that the Basileus is still alive. They go
to the effort of closing the bronze
doors; a furious combat ensues;
Aboulfaradj speaks of 70 guards
killed. At one point even, one might
think that the conspirators are done
for when, by the order of Tzimiskes
who had already rushed into the great
hall of the Chrysotriclinium *so as to*
have himself crowned, Atzypotheodor-
os severs the head of the dead emper-
or and, brandishing it from a window,
displays it in the light of the torches of
the people who had gathered outside.
What a scene, what an exhibition in
that place, on that black night, in that
snow storm! The frightened multitude,
lifting their eyes every which way in
the direction of the dark mass of build-
ings that constituted the Boukoleon,
noticed only a single point of light that
attracted their attention; it was that
group of men vividly lit up by smoking
torches, holding and waving by its
long, black hair, the great basileus
Nicephorus' head, dripping with

blood.

At that sight, the mercenary soldiers, who had believed that their emperor was still alive, stopped in their tracks. Men of a different race, animated by a feeling of military honor completely vanished among the Greeks of the Late Roman Empire, those warriors of the North, hated by a people whom they did not love at all, know that it is all over now, that nobody will follow them if they seek to oppose a revolution already done; they would have valiantly defended Nicephorus, but they will not avenge him.

John Tzimiskes who, during this tumult, has quickly donned the purple boots and adorned himself in the principal attributes of imperial costume, seated on the throne of the Basileis in the splendid Chrysotriclinium, is proclaimed emperor at once by the conspirators and the crowd of his new partisans. Byzantium has changed master!

... All day the following day, Saturday, December 11, in dark and foggy weather, with infinite sadness, the decapitated body of the illustrious vanquisher of the Saracens, thrown from a window into the Palace gardens, re-

mained lying in the snow. Towards evening only, the new sovereign gave an order to make those importunate remains disappear. One could not think, in the confusion of the moment and after that almost public murder, to give the defunct Basileus a proper burial. His inhumation was shamefully clandestine and rushed. That poor body was hastily placed on an improvised stretcher made of branches that were collected here and there and, night having fallen, it was a night of black and thick darkness, they transported him, almost running, without any pomp, in greatest secret, to Saint-Apostles. He was forthwith buried in one of the great sarcophaguses of Constantine's heroon.

John Tzimiskes, The Two Bardas, Basil II's Early Years

I am surely the only contemporary who has read four times this so-called first tome of the *Byzantine Epic* which is, in reality, the second tome, Nicephorus Phocas having been the veritable inaugurator of that Epic which lasted exactly sixty-five years, much to the Muslim world's terror and despair. And I have done this reading not for zeal but in order to *assuage my passions*.

It is certain that right after the very dark drama that terminated Nicephorus' reign, the history of his successor is astonishing. One forgets the horror that had just occurred in the Palace of Boukoleon, on that panic night of December, that nameless terror, the infinite abomination of that group of dogged frenetics who hacked at their sovereign, more miserable than a worm writhing at their feet. They were all recompensed, moreover, more or less promptly, exactly as was to occur two hundred years later in the case of the assassins of the Saint Thomas de Canterbury.

> *The pious Leon Diacre emotionally notes that none of Nicephorus' murderers enjoyed the fruit of his crime peacefully. John Tzimiskes, after a glorious but rather short reign, per-*

ished, he also, by a violent and myste-
rious death. Theophano, chased al-
most immediately from the Palace on
the day after, by her lover and accom-
plice who refused to marry her, led a
lamentable existence going from one
monastery to another, as far as Arme-
nia. The other conspirators, without
exception, met an unfortunate end. Di-
vine justice laid its hand on each one
of them. Only Leon Balantes was exe-
cuted right afterwards for having giv-
en the first stroke. He was the scape-
goat who initially paid for everyone.
John Tzimiskes could not or did not
want to save him.

It does not matter: that Tzimiskes is so handsome a prince that he makes people forget the most
recent past and does not allow them to think of the future, however near. Then he washes his hands so thor-
oughly of the blood of the "just" Nicephorus, in the
blood of his people's enemies, that nobody knows
any longer whether he had soaked them in that of his
emperor or not.

A long time before the crime, before Nicephorus was basileus even, the name of this warrior was
already a symbol of terror in the all the lands held by
Arabs and, from the banks of the Tigris to those of the
Nile, says the chronicler, Saracen mothers frightened
their indocile children by threatening them with the
wrath of the terrible "Tchumuschtiguin." xThe history

of those times, so stingy of documents, has however conserved the story of the battle of the "Mountain of Blood," on the road from Tarsus to Mopsuestia in Cilicia, where one had seen real rivers of blood running in cascades along the hillsides.

The physical contrast, moreover, was crushing for the satyr who had just been replaced on the throne of Constantine.

> *I have recounted, said Schlumberger, his glorious campaigns in the war with the Saracens, the active and preponderant role that he had played in Nicephorus' rise in the Empire, at the time of that military sedition in Caesarea in Cappadocia, which he was the veritable artisan of. I have mentioned his fine qualities of valiance and generosity, kindness, gentleness, uprightness, commonsense, which made him so popular, his admirable quality as a warrior, his incomparable spirit that made him into perhaps the most brilliant personification of military virtues of that epoch and the defender of the most formidable Empire against the Saracens. I have given, after descriptions by contemporaries, an idea of his so characteristic physical portrait, I have painted him as charming, elegant, and noble, with his blue eyes, his alert and good looks, his*

blond hair turning red, his fawn-red colored beard, his very clear complexion, his fine and gently-curved nose, his so well-shaped body of small stature, composed of vigor, agility, and prodigious address; he was the best knight, the best archer, the best javelin thrower in the Empire. He had all the enchanting qualities that allow great crimes to be pardoned and forgotten, all the so amiable vices that people excuse so easily. "He loved wine too much and good food," said Leon Diacre, who knew him, "he ardently loved pleasure and indulged in all its prodigalities." Manasses compares him to a new paradise whence flow the four rivers of justice, wisdom, prudence, and valor. "If he had not soiled his hands," he exclaims, "in Nicephorus' murder, he would have shone in the firmament like an incomparable star." He was the veritable seductive, energetic, and warrior prince that was needed for the restoration of the Empire so gloriously inaugurated by Nicephorus.

It is true that while waiting for the tottering justice that was to settle accounts with him, the Armenian was immediately given two masters.

To begin with, the old patriarch Polyeucte

without whose consecration Tzimiskes knew perfectly well that he could never be considered as anything other than the worst of usurpers. That enraged pontiff made him pay very dearly for his orthodox oil: "I cannot," he told him, "receive into the bosom of the Church anyone whose hands are tainted with that illustrious blood. Before anything, you must do penitence, wash yourself of the capital accusation that weighs on you. Public opinion affirms your participation in Nicephorus' murder. We need the guilty parties. If you want to enter into the Holy Place, there where only I can consecrate you, exonerate yourself to begin with; supposing you succeed, denounce without hesitation the true assassins, whoever they are." He terminated this apostrophe with a phrase that surpasses all those that proceeded it in audacity: "Before anything, chase from the sacred Palace the adulterous and criminal woman who conceived everything, directed everything, and who was clearly the principal guilty party!" There were quite a few other exigencies the least of which was complete abandonment of the Tzimiskes' personal fortune and real property.

Then, the parakoimomenos – or chief minister – Basil, bastard son of the basileus Romanos Lekapenos who had made him a eunuch from early childhood. "They had the custom still," said Lebeau, "of suppressing in that way, in Byzantium, aspirations to the purple of those who, born on the steps of the throne, were however not destined to mount it."

The parakoimomenos Basil had already played, under three successive reigns, a dazzling role. That bold and prudent man, of extraordinary energy, but corrupt, hard, and scrupulous, avid for power to an extraordinary degree, is certainly one of the most interesting and most curious figures of his epoch. Psellus was alone in recounting for us this detail that he was, despite his sad situation of a eunuch, of the most noble presence, of the finest stature, with the most majestic and imposing attitude, as a veritable son of the basileus that he was. His importance, already considerable, for many long years, was going to increase even more under this reign. Under the following reign finally, he was to become, for some time, the first person of the Empire. I will mention in a few words that this celebrated man of State of the second half of the tenth century in the east was the bastard son of the basileus Romanos Lekapenos and a Scythian, that is to say Bulgar or Russian, slave. Ancient favorite of the basileus Constantine Porphyrogenitus, who happened to be his brother-in-law, he had already filled under that prince extremely important functions. He was disorganized, fickle, adventurous, but audacious, very resolute, very opinionated, with a war-

rior's humor, despite his physical con-
dition... In 958 notably, at the head of
all the Anatolian forces, he had
trounced the Saracens and celebrated
a triumph in Constantinople.

The new emperor, who owed to him, in large part, his elevation to the throne, had to have seen that great sterile figure pass sometimes before his mind when he meditated on death.

Pointless to mention the two other basileis, the two sons of Romanos II and Theophano: Basil, aged fourteen years, nicknamed later the Bulgaroctone, and Constantine, aged twelve years, who could not be the masters of anyone. Nicephorus had been the tutor of those two legitimate heirs of the illustrious house of Macedonia, and Tzimiskes was simple going to continue. Since the death of their father, Nicephorus' immediate predecessor, one had dreamt of this thing, seen in Byzantium so many times before: several emperors occupying the imperial throne at the same time, a disastrous state that was to last sixty years.

All concessions having been made, the intractable patriarch having been satisfied in every way, the parakoimomenos having become the first man of state after the "Apostles' Equal," the splendid and desperate Theophano having been transformed over night into a poor woman religious sent to a distant convent; Tzimiskes, crowned finally and free to move about as he pleased, precipitously rallied the Empire's forces.

There was not one hour to lose. The unbridled Russian torrent, unblocked from its ices and from its deserts, emancipated by a mortal imprudence by Nicephorus, was menacing Constantinople, terribly. Legacy of the assassinated Basileus! Never had they been in such great peril. The Russians, or Rus, called Varangos at that time, and of Scandinavian origin very probably, were the Greeks' worst nightmare.

> *The most formidable, the most imme-*
> *diate danger, it was the Russian ene-*
> *my. That ferocious enemy, drunk on its*
> *recent victories over the Bulgar peo-*
> *ple, remained, at that moment, camped*
> *out on the northern frontier, at the foot*
> *of the Balkans, several steps away*
> *from the capital. From one day to the*
> *next its infinite hordes could appear at*
> *the foot of the ramparts of the City*
> *protected by God, supreme goal of*
> *their covetousness... The danger was*
> *immense, imminent, but John Tz-*
> *imiskes, worthy successor of Nicepho-*
> *rus Phocas, was up to the task of those*
> *cruel circumstances.*

> *... One day, around the month of*
> *March, 970, I think, they suddenly re-*
> *ceived frightening news in the City*
> *protected by God. The Russians had*
> *unexpectedly crossed the Balkans.*
> *Like wolves, they had thrown them-*
> *selves on Philippopolis, great and*

strong place built on the Hebrus river, which was at that time part of the Bulgar kingdom. It was the first city encountered by them on the southern side of the mountains. They had taken it and drowned it in a horrible bloodbath. Leon Diacre recounts how 20,000 defenders of the city, taken after victory, were impaled on rows of pikes or hung from rows of gallows by those demons of the North... The panic in Constantinople had to have been extreme.... However, before definitively engaging in desperate battle, John Tzimiskes, all the while rallying his last battalions, wanted to attempt a negotiation. He offered money to the barbarian chief demanding immediate evacuation. Furious, Sviatoslav gave the insolent response that one might imagine. He declared that he would consent to evacuate only the lands of Thrace which he had invaded and only on the condition that the Basileus paid him for those districts as well as for the countless prisoners he had taken, an enormous ransom, but that he was going to set himself up purely and simply in Bulgaria, on the other side of the Danube. "If you don't accept my propositions," he said in a kind of peroration, "you will have no other

choice, you and your subjects, but to
leave Europe once and for all. Go into
Asia, abandon Constantinople to us."

Thus did the prince of the Rus, Sviatoslav, son of Igor, prince of Kiev, the "mother of Russian cities," say to John Tzimiskes. It was the third time in a century, since the miraculous defeat of Askold the Varango driven off by Photius, dipping the divine *maphorion* in the waves, that the Russians so audaciously ordered the secular possessors of Byzantium to evacuate the queen City for their benefit. "Alas!" adds Schlumberger, "so many times in the future until our days, their descendants had to renew the same menaces, and nevertheless the Moscovite race has not yet occupied the famous spaces where formerly the sacred Palace of the emperors of Rum was erected!"

War was inevitable and merciless. No grace to be expected from those ferocious brutes absolutely unworthy of pardon. "Not content," says the honest Lebeau, "to set farms, villages, churches on fire, they made a game out of the most inhuman tortures. They put the inhabitants on a cross, piercing others with a javelin and leaving them staked to the ground; others bound to posts served as a target for their arrows. Their cruelty gave distinction to priests and clerics; after having bound their hands behind their back, they diverted themselves by embedding nails into their skull..."

I really hope that it is in this way that the Prussians treat us in their next war. They often demonstrated, in 1870, that their inclination is such.

Yes, I would like to see those renegade Lutherans, more criminal and accursed in their souls than pagans even, to take it to the limit because then, doubtless, a Christian France would finally rise up, for their extermination, from that teeming of horrors.[12]

One must insist on the singularly diabolical character of that Russo-Greek war of the tenth century, today so profoundly forgotten, compared to which it seems that the Russo-Turkish war of 1877 was like a series of benign slayings. It is indisputable that John Tzimiskes was a savior, and the savior of how many peoples! Sviatoslav was for Byzantium the same menace and the same danger that Alaric was for Rome in the fifth century, and his great army, the newest, most intact there was in the world, was also at that time the most terrifying that could be imagined.

> *Listen to this description, by a modern author, of the bands that accompanied Oleg, the predecessor of Sviatoslav, in his attack on Constantinople, sixty years before that. That enumeration (which recalls the* Legend of the Centuries[13]*) could be applied as well to the no less redoubtable bands that Sviatoslav brought with him: "Beside the gigantic Scandinavian foot soldiers, – the Varangos or Russians properly speaking, the Tauroscytes according*

[12]Original footnote: Written in 1906.

[13]*Legend of the Centuries*: a famous book of poetry by Victor Hugo.

*to Byzantine historians, dressed in
iron, armed with swords, in both
hands, and with the formidable dou-
ble-headed axe, – beside them
marched the civilized Slavs of Nov-
gorod, Smolensk, and Kiev, with their
blue eyes and blond hair, armed with
German lances and Damascened
glaives; the savage Slavs of the
forests, Drevlians, Radimitches,
Tivertses, Khrobates, half-naked,
wearing sandals and holding poisoned
arrows in their hands or the leather
lasso with which they dragged their
enemies away; the Finnish of White
Lake and the upper Volga, with their
savage looks, fiery hair, and an earth-
brown complexion to their skin,
dressed in bear hides and carrying
heavy clubs on their shoulders; the
Tchoudes horsemen of Finland and
Estonia, caracoling on their small
horses and trying out their enormous
Lapland bows along the way; the
Bjarmians from the gulf of Arkhangel-
sk, proud of their golden rings and
their Turkish sabres bought from the
Bulgars; finally, attracted by the hope
for gain, some Finnish Gvenes from
Lake Vleo, veritable giants redoubted
for their strength and their somber energy, whose secular quarrels with the*

Scandinavians are symbolized in the mythology of the North by the battles of giants against the Æsir.

The fervor of those barbarian masses was like the shaking of Hell's columns. "The Varangos as well as the Normans," says Alfred Rambaud, "surprised the people of the Midi by their temerarious bravery and their gigantic stature." "They were as tall as palm trees," say the Arabs. Audacious mariners, admirable foot soldiers, the Varangos greatly differed from the mounted peoples and nomads of southern Russia, Hungarians, Khazars, Pechenegs, who didn't know how to fight except by fleeing. The Russians, according to Leon Diacre, who had seen them at work, battling in a compact mass and looking like a bronze mural, bristling with lances, glimmering for the shine of their shields, whence came a sustained clamor, a roaring like that of the sea, the famous *barditus* or *barritus* of the Germans in Tacitus, that terrible song of war "which made those who heard it die for fear, including the birds in the skies." "Never, in a defeat," says the same author, "did one see them give up. When they despaired of victory, they shredded their own entrails."

Finally, their multitude seemed innumerable. But, once again, there was John Tzimiskes who could have said, like Napoleon: "Fifty thousand men and me, that makes one hundred fifty thousand men."

Warned by his scouts that the Russians neglected to place guards in the dangerous passes of the Balkans, John sees the entire event of the war in a flash and decides instantly to profit by that enormous error, without losing an hour. Rapidly, he communicates his plan to his shuddering officers. The Balkans had a bad reputation in Byzantium. Its name recalled terrible disasters. Nobody however is bold enough to gainsay the autocrator whose magnanimous assurance lifts all courage. The army set off all together. This resembles a dream.

> *At its head marched the troop of immortals, a creation by John Tzimiskes, famous cavalry who were going to be covered in glory in this war. That splendid elite body, that sort of imperial phalange, had been recruited with care from among the young nobles, from among the most tested and intrepid soldiers of the armies of Anatolia... According to Leon Diacre, that must have been an extraordinary sight, the marching past of that brilliant troop of men, cuirassed, sparkling in gold and silver.*

> *Behind them the Basileus, surrounded by the most brilliant chief of staff. He had put on, so tells us the chronicler, a marvelous suit of armor that covered him from head to foot... The dazzling display of the costumes and the richness of the arms were for the leaders, at that time, a powerful means of acting on the simple souls of those war-*

like multitudes, as well on those who combatted under their orders and those whom they were going to fight. In order for the general to be unquestionably obeyed, he had to appear in a quasi divine radiation, like a being above humanity, resplending with the fire of metal, gleaming with the most beautiful of colors, like a sort of supernatural combatant... John's magnificent horse must have been covered in gold, perhaps silk, with precious gems or sometimes cameos in the guise of phalera. From a distance, the Basileus shone under the Balkan sun like a legendary Saint Georges.

Thirty thousand belligerents followed his magnificence, and all that was merely an avant guard.

As he had announced to his lieutenants, the redoubted pass was left unencumbered. After having crossed the mountain and after several hours of rest, they marched in close columns on the great Pereyaslavets, the old capital of the Bulgar tsars, site of war defended by a notable party of the Russian army. The siege, begun on Holy Wednesday, was completed on the following day, by extermination of the besieged.

At the probable hour when Our Lord Jesus Christ, ready to suffer the Passion, had said to his Apostles, "This is my body, this is my blood," there were in that city in flames, 8,000 *bodies* of the sons of the giants of the steppe, lying in their own *blood*.

The victorious army rested on Good Friday and the two following days, so that on Easter Sunday the Emperor and his soldiers celebrated, in the half-ruined basilica of the old Bulgar capital, the Feast of the Resurrection.

But the bulk of their work was as yet to be done. Sviatoslav was in Dorystolon (Silistra), on the Danube, with 60,000 warriors. Tzimiskes, who had wanted Bulgaria to be the Russians' grave, had made his fleet go up river of the Danube to cut off any retreat, Dorystolon being on the right bank of that river which was called Ister at that time.[14] That fleet was a monster for the Russians, and it was almost enough on sight to throw them into despair. The way to safety and escape over the Danube was now definitively taken away from those barbarians. Their terror seems also to have been extreme. They knew that the sides of those boats contained liquid fire, the terror of their nation. "Since childhood," says Leon Diacre, "in their distant huts, they had all shuddered with fear on hearing their fathers tell how the Median flames had destroyed, on the Black Sea, the immense number of

---

[14]Original footnote: Leon Diacre informs us seriously that this was one of the rivers that flowed from Terrestrial Paradise, "that which had the name of Physon." Leaving Eden in the East, it went underground and, after having flowed for some time, rose again to the surface of the earth, near the Celtic mountains, from which it flowed through Europe, to throw itself through five mouths into the Black Sea. Such was, towards the end of the third quarter of the tenth century, the state of geographical knowledge of a Byzantine priest, one of the most erudite, one of the most literate of his time.

small boats making up the fleet of Igor, their prince's father."

There was not a single Russian house-hold that had not lost a family mem-ber, burned or drowned; and in the evening, in their vigils, in Scythia, on the high hills surrounding Kiev, or on the low-lying banks of the sonorous porogues *of the old Dnieper, old peo-ple described to distraught young peo-ple the terrible burns caused by the di-abolical engine that nobody could ex-tinguish, whose wet flames ran along the surface of the waters as over the naked body of the warriors. One imag-ines what could have been Svi-atoslav's soldiers' emotion. Recalling in haste their scattered boats which covered the course of the river, their familiar boats, each one cut out of a single tree trunk, so lightweight that they were carried alongside the rapids, those loyal dugouts that had helped them come so far, descending the course of their national rivers; they probably pulled them up onto dry land under the walls of the city, there where the Danube ran at the foot of the rampart. From the heights of the crenelations they constantly launched onto the river a rain of arrows and stones, hoping to prevent the Byzan-*

tine vessels from drawing close enough to burn those boats that remained, in spite of everything, their one hope of escape.

Thus Dorystolon offered, in the spring of the year 972, the formidable and curious spectacle of those two armies, of those two so dissimilar fleets brought together under its walls. Very few great military scenes have been able to garner more poignant interest. At the center, Silistra with its high ramparts bristling with towers peopled by defenders, with its streets, its squares covered by gigantic warriors with raucous and sonorous voices, strange warriors from the Scythian ices, frightening brutes wearing mail; around them, the captive Pechenegs, Hungarians, Bulgars, "all the peoples of the Horde," dressed in animal hides. To the south, the vast camp of the Byzantine army swarming with thousands of soldiers made up of many races, the long scintillation of that prodigious wall of shields and lances thrust into the ground, the moving about of cataphract cavalries, the marches and countermarches of foot soldiers making up the investment of troops, the superb costumes worn by the Basileus and his chiefs, the stun-

ning troop of immortals. To the north, the dark Danube flowing slowing through its dark valley, the Russian boats by the hundreds, perhaps thousands, lined up on the bank like a flock of animals: farther away, in a vast half circle, the igniferous Greek fleet with their silk ensigns, their colored sails, the costumes of its thousands of sailors, tightly blocking the enemy dugouts, observing them relentlessly in order to bar their retreat. In the distance, the infinite plain, barren and gloomy, as far as the fogs of Scythia, and perhaps, even farther, some wandering band of Hungarian knights come to pillage, attracted like vultures by the odor of carnage, contemplating while surprised, from atop their meager mounts, the unprecedented spectacle. [15]

This new siege lasted more than three months. There were Homeric battles, very dangerous peripeteias. One day the megalomartyr saint Theodore Stratelates in person, one of two military saints of that name, nicknamed Calliniques, was

---

[15]Original footnote: Although a lampoonist by profession, according to what people say, I would have little self-respect if I didn't express my admiration for this superb page that seems to me entirely of the first order. My readers know that I don't answer to anyone, and that I cannot be in any way the personal flatterer of Gustave Schlumberger whose views, sometimes, I am far from sharing, and from whom I expect nothing.

obliged to intervene in order to give victory to the
Byzantines, for it is common knowledge that the orthodox could count on the assistance of Paradise in
the extreme case of need, which would certainly not
have been possible for the Christians of the West who
obeyed the Pope.

The barbarians continued to give themselves
up, to leave off all arrogance, to consider themselves
happy not to have been massacred to the last man and
to recover with difficulty, with the alms of bread giv-
en to them by the Basileus and several thousand
wounded, the mouths of the faraway Dnieper, where
the lice-eating Pechenegs finished them off. Thus did
that atrocious war end, for the great glory of Tzimiskes, who splendidly triumphed in Constantinople.

Russia, which had only just been recently
born, continued its destiny which appeared to be that
of receiving from the Greeks, not only the blows, but
its laws, its mores, is architecture, its autocracy, its
language even, and above all its atrophied religion
which it was dying of for a thousand years. One
knows that in 989, the princess Anna, daughter of Romanos II and sister of the two reigning basileis, was
married politically to the terrible Vladimir, the fratricidal bastard with eight hundred concubines, and that
it is then that Russia became Christian, the awful
Christian that it has always been.

> *Alas! the stories of poor princesses
> sacrificed for reasons of State are a
> recurring theme throughout history,
> but are there many whose fate was*

more lamentable? What a tragic, immense contrast between the brilliant and sweet existence she had in Constantinople and that which the Porphyrogenita was going to lead going forward!... She left in order to become the spouse of a ferocious and debauched chief, the worshiper of frightening idols, who, most certainly, would not convert to the Gospel of peace except in word only. She was going to reign, not over a nation of knights, of bourgeois, of artisans and priests, but over savage populations with violent customs, with uniquely warlike passions, huddled together in agglomerations of sordid huts pompously decorated with the name of cities. She was going to live among those terrible barbarians, "the filthiest men God has created," as Ibn Fozlan exclaimed, who visited them in 922.

They were no different in 1814. They haven't budged since, and what madness to hope that those Scythians who were kept for ten centuries in the most abject slavery, in order to be suddenly set free, are going to govern themselves wisely, kissing the hands and feet of a *constitutional autocrat![16]*

The war against the Russians had been longer and more difficult that Tzimiskes had anticipated, be-

---

[16]Original footnote: one is reminded that this was written in 1906.

cause of the concomitant and unexpected revolt by Bardas Phocas, nephew of the defunct basileus Nicephorus. That revolt, promptly put down, was the beginning of that prodigious chassé-croisé of false emperors fighting one against the other alternately, which lasted nearly twenty years, which nearly succeeded in ruining the Empire and which is a unique thing in history. Bardas Phocas, immensely redoubtable man of war, one of so many whom the Byzantine tenth century knew how to produce, was a great lord in Cappadocia, vast mountainous and central theme from which all the Phocas originated. He had counted on the immense difficulty of the Russian war, and the situation had appeared so grave in the Holy Palace that the departure of the Basileus and his army towards the north had been countermanded. Delay that could lose everything and that made the situation two times more tragic.

Tzimiskes, fortunately, in order to oppose that rebel, had an adversary worthy of him, another Bardas who had just then vanquished the Russians in a first engagement of the vanguard. Bardas Skleros' sword blows would have surprised Richard the Lionheart himself if that blowhard from Ptolemais or Jaffa could see him. The duel was short but, by the Emperor's decision, much more political than bloody. In a few days, Bardas Skleros, invested with plenary powers, furnished with imperial letters sealed by golden bull and brevets in white, awarding him the dignities of stratigos, patrician, etc..., succeeded in enticing away the principal adherents of the usurper. The latter, nearly abandoned by everyone, is reduced to taking flight and to giving himself up soon afterwards. The compassionate Tzimiskes merely ordered that he be relegated to the island of Chio with his family. Quite a soft punishment and surprising for a Byzantine prince.

Leaving the septentrional frontier of Bulgaria to the protection of the savage Paulician heretics transplanted there expressly and whom our historian has the extreme goodness of admiring, Tzimiskes was finally able to bring his thoughts back, all his warrior energy, towards the Saracen East forever teeming with menaces, towards those provinces of upper Syria, northern Phoenicia and Cilicia which had only recently been reconquered by Nicephorus against the eternal Mussulman enemy. Profoundly humiliated, the latter dreamt of nothing else than vengeance, in Egypt, Arabia, Persia and all meridional Syria. Antioch even had been insulted. A Roman army had been exterminated beneath the walls of Amid which is Diyarbakir and its leaders, forty in number, sent as captives to Bagdad where they died. It was time that the infidels felt the heavy hand of the Basileus of Rum on the nape of their neck again.

> *The hereditary enemy came at that very moment to assemble a new, immense force with the establishment of the al-Mu'izz Fatimid empire erected on the debris of the Ikhshidids' sovereignty. The Egyptian armies, which had barely counted under the most recent basileis, had suddenly be-*

come redoubtable; they could now, from one day to the next, retake the offensive in the holy war, capable of fighting with advantage against the best imperial troops... Already they had reentered Damascus. That new power could not, without posing infinite danger, be allowed to grow like that and draw near to the Empire's frontiers... The present anarchy of the Caliphate of Bagdad would need to be taken advantage of in order to prevent and forbid in that city, as in Aleppo as well, all restoration of a strongly centralized power... At all costs, that precise moment needed to be taken advantage of in order to finish the work so valiantly begun by Nicephorus, in order definitively to beat the moribund eastern Caliphate and to try to make all Muslim Middle East a part of the empire or at least the land of a vassal. John Tzimiskes, in his bellicose vigils in the Sacred Palace, thought of nothing else and, it must be said, that politic of bold and immediate conquest was, in some sort, imposed on him by the circumstances. It was the religious idea, so powerful in Byzantium, that drove him in that direction with every last vigor. Jerusalem, the Holy City, goal of ardent desire by so many mil-

lions of pious souls, already at that time the center of fervent pilgrimages, the unique City towards which all Christianity turned its gaze, groaning under the cruel yoke of the lieutenants of the Fatimids. It seemed of every necessity that a basileus full of piety, a "philochrist" emperor, as one said in Byzantium, should go and deliver the Savior's City from its chains. Such were the pious and glorious projects that rolled through the head of that heroic and crowned Armenian, vanquisher of the Russians, dominator of the Bulgars. Those projects, Nicephorus Phocas, no less heroic, had nourished them before him... "John Tzimiskes' plan," said Lebeau, "was envisioned more than one hundred years in advance of the Crusades."

Before going any further, let us listen to Schlumberger's almost continual complaint about the excessive aridity of historical sources with respect to the reign of Tzimiskes and above all the reign of Basil II who succeeded him. "It is," he says, "the period of utter poverty of sources, of endless lacuna, of complete darkness. No expression would know how to give a just idea of a like dearth of documents... I have gone through hundreds of volumes and memoirs to find sometimes three lines of intelligence, if I am lucky. This meticulous mosaic work has cost me an immense amount of trouble, thousands and thousands of hours of work."

What is certain is that huge events have been completely, I do not say lost, but *hidden*, which is more or less afflicting. That depends on what God has put in one's heart and the idea that one has of history. We know something however. There is no period in its history of a certain length about which we do not know at least some facts, which is, if you will, a kind of miracle in such a swallowing up. One has to wonder what that would that be like for an entire century that one knew absolutely nothing about? What to think, for example, of a history of France that stopped brusquely, inexorably, at the Battle of Malplaquet only to pick up again with the ashes of Napoleon, without there remaining the possibility of a hypothesis in order to shed light on such a gulf? Eh well! that would change nothing for divine Life which is the only history, and that would change nothing either in that intangible certitude that, being "images" of God, we are called to know everything. *Everything* that is fulfilled on earth will be put before our eyes when it is necessary, before our true invisible and imperishable eyes, and that will be a dazzling display of Paradise finally to learn why certain things were not shown to us before. It is probable that we pass by the Tree of Knowledge of good and evil every day, without even seeing it, and that is assuredly an inestimable benefit. But God, who has pity on our curious souls, permits some fruits to be three-quarters eaten by worms and gathered up in the shade by impatient souls like Schlumberger who do not have the courage to wait for the beatific vision, and it is in this way that this historian was able to write enormous volumes, interesting like beautiful heroic poems, on Nicephorus, Tzimiskes, and Basil II.

There were two great expeditions by Tzimiskes in Asia. One knows precious little about the first one, if not that he first led his soldiers into Armenia where he struck an alliance with the Bagratid king, Aschot III, the Merciful. The story told by Mathieu of Edessa is not very clear, and I confess to have never been able, even with Schlumberger's assistance, to make any sense of the horribly complicated affairs of the Armenian or Georgian kings or dynasties which greatly preoccupied the basileis. That great people, easily heroic, but always divided and ungovernable, greatly resembles Poland which had a cruel destiny, having been consumed in the end by the Russians and by the Turks, without hope of resurrection. I have understood more from the beautiful engravings, numerous reproductions of photographs of the ruins of Ani, the former, famous capital of the king of kings of Armenia, which the conscientious historian of the *Epic* examined with devotion.

Having settled his Armenian affairs, I do know so much how, Tzimiskes "like an ardent flame," says Mathieu d'Edessa, invaded Mesopotamia.

> There was, as always, a terrible destruction of the unfortunate countrysides, a terrifying devastation. The incredible richness of those blessed lands, inundated by the sun, is re-

quired to explain how, after so many wars of extermination, those provinces could continue, each year, to nourish their inhabitants. They razed to the ground three hundred towns and fortresses as far as the confines of Bagdad... Conquering again northern Mesopotamia, after having entirely ravaged it and momentarily subjected it, he wanted, he too, to try that grandiose adventure that had already seduced many other basileis before him, many other Byzantine captains. He resolved, the sources at any rate seem to indicate it, to march on that opulent and mysterious Bagdad, capital of the eastern Caliphate, center of the Muslim world in Asia, prestigious city, "never yet pillaged," where all the treasures of the East were piled up for more than two centuries since the city had been founded by Caliph Abu Ja'far al-Mansur. The ardent Basileus clearly understood what a terrible blow he could deal to Muhammad's strength if he succeeded in laying his hands on it.

He had only, it seemed, but to extend his hand. Why didn't he do it? Silence and darkness.

John Tzimiskes, probably leaving his army in the cantonments of Tarsus and

Antioch, made a triumphal entry into Constantinople. In addition to much glory, the Basileus returned with an immense amount of booty. Carried before him were "300 myriads," or 3 million pieces of gold and silver money, "300,000 pounds of gold and silver," says Leon Diacre. That was the second triumph of that reign, which was merely however at its aurora, splendid triumph through all the acclamations and euphemies of an innumerable population. The cortege of Saracen captives, precious metals, gold-threaded stuffs, perfumes, aromatics, Eastern weapons, was of an immense richness. We know nothing more about it.

One would be perhaps even more poorly informed on the second expedition without the recent find of an inestimable document, a long authentic letter by John Tzimiskes to his ally, the sovereign Bagratid of Armenia. "This imperial letter, abundant in unpublished facts of the most vivid interest, is an official bulletin as veridical as it is detailed on the campaign of 975 in Syria and the dazzling triumphs carried out by the Basileus and his loyal troops over the Mussulmen, the bulletin signed by that great man himself." One must read it in its entirety. It is as if a miraculous window onto the earthly Paradise of historians, that is to say very obscure epochs that no one can penetrate.

By means of this happy document, Schlumberger has forced himself to reconstitute the exact itinerary of the imperial army in Syria and Palestine. Seeing this veritable recitation in the light of several accessory bits of information furnished by chroniclers, one can follow, almost step by step, the conqueror from Membdj, the ancient Hierapolis on the Euphrates and, passing through the opulent Apamee, through Emesa, natal city of Heliogabalus, through Balbek with its giant ruins as far as the radiant Damascus, pearl of the East which the king of France and the Holy Roman Emperor were unable to take one hundred sixty years later, but whose keys the emir, before any combat, had handed over to the irresistible Basileus. "For the longest time, no Byzantine emperor had, astride his warhorse, tread over the green fields of that queen of Syrian cities, gently stretching beyond the mountain, among its great gardens. Even Nicephorus had been unable to go so far." Why didn't he keep going to Jerusalem? Same question for Bagdad and the same response. That by Tzimiskes himself is by far insufficient. Here is what he wrote to the king of Armenia:

> From Damascus, we directed ourselves to the Lake of Tiberias, there where our Lord Jesus Christ, with two fish and five loaves of barley, made his miracle. We resolved to assault the city, but the inhabitants came out to us to announce their submission... So we let them free of the yoke of servitude and we abstained from ruining their

city and their territory. We spared them from pillage, because that was the country of the holy Apostles. It was the same thing with Nazareth where the mother of God, the holy Virgin Mary, heard the good News *from the mouth of the angel.*

Having gone to Mount Tabor, we climbed to the location where Christ, our Lord, was transfigured. As we made a stop, people came to us, from Ramla and from Jerusalem, to solicit Our Royalty and implore our mercy. They asked for a leader from among us, recognized themselves as our tributaries, and consented to our domination; we granted their wishes. Our desire was to free the Holy Sepulcher of Christ from the outrages of Mussulmen. We set up our military chiefs in all the themes submissive to us and which had become our tributaries, from Beit She'an, which is also called Decapolis, to Genesareth and to Acre, which is also called Ptolemais. The inhabitants were engaged, by written document, to pay us, each year, a perpetual tribute and to live under our authority. From there, we came to Caesarea which is situated on the shores of the Mediterranean Sea and was captured; and if those cursed

Africans, who had established their residence there, had not taken refuge in the fortresses of the littoral, we would have left, sustained by the help of God, for the holy city of Jerusalem, and we would have been able to pray in those venerable places.

And that's it. The victorious army, greatly in vain it seems, goes back North and the assassin Tzimiskes, repulsed by Jesus Christ, hastens to his destiny. Dolorous and inexplicable peripeteia which history is full of. One knows that God is always adorable, but how to penetrate his actions? Why those brusque interruptions, those sudden abortions? The glory of a Tzimiskes or of a Saint Louis, for example, has the air of humbly corresponding with divine Glory, and then comes God who casts everything to the ground. It is a gulf in which human reason is lost. Tzimiskes was condemned for centuries. He died of poison, it is highly probable, and the poisoner was his old accomplice, the parakoimomenos Basil, that demon of activity and astuteness who had so greatly assisted him in becoming emperor. Such is the tragic tale told by Leon Diacre.

As the army, traversing Cilicia, passed by Anazarbus and Podyandos, the Emperor marveled at the dazzling scene of those fertile countrysides, covered by flocks, rich with all the goods of nature, formerly a possession of the crown, and whose recent conquest had just cost so much blood and pain to the imperial troops. As he was inform-ing himself of the names of the present proprietors of those lands, invariably someone responded to him that they belonged to the parakoimomenos alone. The proedros *Basil was, like all Byzantine men of State at that time, a great hoarder of national goods, which he had attributed to himself un-der all pretexts, with brutal avidity. We are unaware, moreover, by what usurpations the famous minister, hated by the people for his severity, had suc-ceeded in placing his hand on those beautiful domains without John even suspecting it.*

By this time the valiant man of war no longer had for that almighty eunuch the same feelings that he had before, and he was thinking already perhaps of doing without his services, having grown impatient with hearing his name crop up at every instant. Finally, sent over the edge with indignation, he could no longer keep it to himself: "Alas," he exclaimed, "must the most generous blood of our soldiers be spilt twenty times over; must Nicephorus Phocas and myself, with the bravest captains of the Empire, having waged so many glorious battles, assumed so

*many fatigues, met so many evils, –
must it all be for the sole enrichment
of one vile eunuch! For the benefit of
that man, then, nations of the Empire
must be ruined in contributions of
war, imperial armies must fight, emperors themselves must leave on campaigns and go and expose themselves
to danger, beyond the frontiers – for
that one man! These are some admirable lands here. Some were conquered by the glorious Nicephorus,
others by me, others still by illustrious
leaders, and now they must all belong
to that one Basil. So much trouble and
effort merely for the profit of that miserable eunuch! After so many con-
quests, the State has kept nothing for
itself!"*

*Fatal words that must have cost that
emperor his life. The terrible eunuch,
admirably served by his spies, irritated and fearing a disgrace, resolved,
with accustomed decision, to take control of the situation... A slow, but sure
poison, was poured into Tzimiskes'
drink. On the following day, an immense torpor seized him; he found
himself as if paralyzed. His stiff limbs
refused to respond. An interior fire
consumed the unfortunate man. His
sufferings were terrible. His weakness*

grew suddenly extreme. Frightening pustules, bubos covered his shoulders. Blood was coming out of his eyes in streams. All remedies were to no effect. Feeling death come on, the unfortunate man dispatched the order to complete his tomb immediately. Tragic return to Constantinople. Instead of a superb reception prepared with so much love, a scene of universal mourning and despair, atrocious agony in complete triumph. Finally having given everything he had, full of Christian humility and contrition, he gave up the ghost on January 9, 976, aged fifty-one years, after six years thirty days of reign. Thus ended, in the flower of his manhood, the most brilliant, bravest, perhaps best of all Byzantine basileis.

Schlumberger who had formerly prepared for historical criticism by the conscientious study of medical sciences, considers that "slow poison" to be an absurd legend. He would lean rather toward typhus, but he does not come right out and say it. "I leave it to the reader the effort of getting to the bottom of this obscure and difficult question," he said, leaving it at that. That at least consoles me a bit with respect to the death of the hero. When it comes right down to it, Schlumberger is a man who likes to laugh, like all members of the Institute.

But the good Armenian, once interred in his dear oratory attached to the Chalke, consecrated to Christ the Euergetes, where he had had a magnificent tomb constructed for himself, – it was not completely over yet with the parakoimomenos. That eunuch intended to command the entire Empire by himself, while remaining the all-powerful minister and tutor of the young emperors Basil II and Constantine VIII. In fact, he succeeded in hanging on for another ten years, that is until the day when the Bulgar Slayer's claws having grown sufficient to the task, this latter man killed him with one blow.

Here now is a summary of the astonishing history of the two Bardas. In 971, during a full invasion by the Russians, the first revolt by Bardas Phocas, promptly put down by Bardas Skleros, lieutenant and brother-in-law of Tzimiskes. In 976, immediately after the distressing death of that emperor, the first revolt, terrible this one, by Bardas Skleros, exasperated by the injustice and bad treatments made by the parakoimomenos. "Long live the autocrator Bardas Skleros, Beloved of God!" clamored all Asia for three years, from the Euphrates to the Bosphorus. All seemed lost. The parakoimomenos, at the end of his tether, thinks to entrust the repression of that rebel to him whom Skleros had so rapidly disarmed and brought low five years earlier, Bardas Phocas, kept captive since then and gnawing his heart out on the Island of Chios.

His choice of minister was found to be excellent. Bardas Phocas was quite worthy of being the opponent of Skleros. What a strange return, and how these events, alas! so drily, so briefly recounted by the chroniclers, curiously illustrate that history of Byzantium, so fertile in stunning changes of fortune! By a game of fate, nowise rare in that period, those two illustrious personages had, after seven years, exactly changed roles. In 971, Bardas Phocas was the rebel claiming the Empire and Skleros was, in the name of the Basileus, charged with thwarting him. In 978, it was precisely the inverse.

Phocas, horribly beaten two times by Skleros, ended up by beating him the third time with the assistance of the powerful Curopalate of Iberia[17] who had furnished him with a contingent of admirable troops.

That was around the time when the Holy Roman Emperor Otto II of Germany was ravaging France "with such an army that no man had seen before, or that no man had seen anything the like of," had a gigantic *Alleluia* sung on Montmartre to his sixty thousand warriors, and embedded his lance into the portal of Lothar's capital in a mark of defiance.

After the irreparable rout of the Battle of Pankaleia, in the Western theme of the Anatolias, fleet escape by the lost pretender, through Asia Mi-

---

[17]Iberia: Caucasian Iberia, or the kingdom of Georgia – not to be confused with the Iberian peninsula in Europe.

nor, across the Sangarius river, across the Halys river, across the Euphrates, to Bagdad finally where he becomes the Caliph's prisoner for seven years. "The eighth indiction goes from September 1, 979, to August 31, 980, period which corresponds to the first part of Bardas Skleros captivity in Bagdad," according to dates given by Elmacin. "The disruption caused by the Bardas Skleros' frightful revolt had lasted largely four years then, from the spring of the year 976 to the summer of the year 980. During that long period, the unfortunate themes of Asia had been almost constantly a prey to the most terrible anarchy."

The indifference of those great men of the tenth century to the infinite trouble that they caused their contemporaries, their absolute lack of what we call patriotism, is inconceivable for men born in the nineteenth century, before the automobile. To be sure, ambitious men such as those Bardas dogs never entertained a thought about the innumerable human lives sacrificed to their scabious itch to seize total power. The only ill, for them, was not to be emperor.

In a contemporary poem, the fratricidal war of the two Bardas is compared to the battle of the giants. There you have it, all the horror that they inspired. Neither the one, nor the other, moreover, succeeded to the throne, and that alternating sedition that struck a mortal blow to the Empire and had for assistants all the demons of hell – lasted no less than eighteen years!

Let us include here another groan by Schlumberger:

The sources of origin, as much Byzantine as Arabic, that furnish us with these relatively rather numerous indications on the first revolt by Bardas Skleros, during the first four years of Basil II and Constantine VIII's reign, turns into a truly desperate poverty for the years immediately following, from the end of 980 to the spring of 986, epoch of the first great campaign against the Bulgars. As for what transpired during this period of nearly six years, in the capital and in both the Western and Eastern themes, the manner in which the young basileis lived, as well their minister the parakoimomenos and their people, the great and small events that occurred – we know nothing or almost nothing about it!... The history of the empire of Rum is much poorer still in terms of documents compared to the monarchies of Western Europe, for that disinherited period, still so shrouded in mystery, at the end of the tenth century...

Bardas Skleros, given his liberty in 987, had nothing more pressing, of course, than to use the very recent disaster of the imperial army by the Bulgars at the defile from the port of Trajan, to have himself proclaimed basileus once again and such was his second revolt, if one could say even that he had ever stopped being a rebel. That happened in Malatya, on

the extreme frontier of Mesopotamia. Scarcely several months later, same scene in Charisan, not far from
Caesarea in Cappadocia, where the attachment to the
Phocas was hereditary. That made now two basileis in
Asia alone and two more in the sacred Palace.[18] Bardas Phocas, let loose once more against Bardas
Skleros on account of Constantinople's fear, had himself, for the second time, him also, proclaimed by the
leaders of the Asian army. That in utter contempt for
the most formidable oaths sworn over the most distinguished of relics. At the time that Skleros first took
up arms, he must have already sworn the same oaths,
under threat of the most terrible punishments of hell
in the case of perjury. Our historian asks himself
"what is more surprising, that ardent ambition of
those captains constantly occupied in a struggle for
supreme power, or the naïvety of the times which still
supposes some efficacity in those oaths of a day constantly retaken, always transgressed anew."

How did Skleros, who was already a rather
old wildcat, let himself be taken in by that immensely
crude ruse by his enemy who proposed to unite together with him to fight against the two young emperors, offering in the case of victory to abandon all of
Asia to him, while he held on to Constantinople and
the European themes?

---

[18]Original footnote: Not too long before this time, at the beginning
of July, in the beautiful cathedral of Noyon, the archbishop
Adalberon of Reims had placed on the head of Hughes Capet,
duke of France, that royal crown that had been lost to the
declining race of Charlemagne and which his descendants were
to pass down throughout so many centuries. The last French
King of Carolingian race, Louis V, died in Senlis on May 21, 987.

Phocas, who seems to have been much superior to him in astuteness, had him taken by surprise and locked up in a hereditary fortress of his family's where he himself, – unusual turn of fate! – besieged in 971, had been forced to give himself up to the same Skleros, now fallen in turn into his hands by the most hateful of betrayals.

The denouement is near. Entirely eternal as he is, God, as well as men, seems to have had enough. Phocas the perfidious, sure of triumph, marches towards the Bosphorus at the head of a powerful army. "All Asia," says Leon Diacre, "all maritime cities and ports belonged to Phocas, except Abydos. Having brought together a fleet of galleys, he held the Hellespont straits with them, barring the passage to ships loaded with grain for the provisioning of the capital."

The situation of the Macedonian dynasty seemed almost desperate. In Asia, Bardas Phocas was really all-powerful. His troops, not content with blocking the faubourgs of Constantinople, tightened their grip around the last city that had remained in imperial hands, on the meridional coast of the straits, starving that immense city. In Europe, the Bulgars, completely victorious following the catastrophe of the preceding year, occupied a large part of the themes and menaced all the rest. Of these two perils, Bardas Phocas was certainly the more pressing...

The young Basileus Basil, the future Bulgar Slayer, saved Byzantium by his decision and his admirable promptitude. He knew to call and lead in time to Constantinople the top warriors in the world, having taken into his pay the bands of the Great Prince of Russia, Vladimir, the savage son of Sviatoslav. Assistance bought through the more or less voluntary sacrifice of the poor princess Anna, sister of the Basileus, to the horrible Vladimir, infinitely sad marriage that was the deplorable occasion of the conversion of the Russians to the Greek schism.

The extraordinary event on the plain of Abydos made only partial use of that assistance so dearly paid for. The two armies were in each other's presence for several days. The pretender, already exasperated by a first setback, noticing Basil who was galloping in front of his troops, animating them to combat, was transported by a fury that made him seem possessed. "Considering," says the chronicler, "that if he could kill him, he would easily get the better of those who were following him, preferring besides a glorious death to the shame of defeat," that man, congested with rage, made mad and poisoned by his sacrilegious oaths, decided to make one last attempt or die in the act. A large empty space separated them. In a furious gallop that nothing seemed able to stop, like that of the "clouds pushed by a violent storm," he rushed headlong at the Emperor. He was about to reach him when suddenly, to the indescribable astonishment of everyone, he was seen to turn around as if taken by vertigo, do an about-face with his horse, climb up a hill at full gallop, then fall to the ground, lie in the dirt, and die not long thereafter. Zonaras affirms that no trace of a wound could be found on his body, circumstance which gives way to infinite hypotheses.

The civil war had been brought to a close at once without the eternal Skleros having been given his liberty, on account of Phocas' widow who wanted to avenge her husband's death. That indefatigable old man, grouping around himself the very formidable remainder of his rival's dispersed army, adopted, as the consummate captain that he was, a new and desperate tactic.

> *Obstinately refusing to give battle, recounts Psellus, avoiding with extreme care any encounter with the main body of the imperial forces, incessantly occupied in recruiting partisans, swelling his ranks, he waged partisan warfare against Basil and his lieutenants, destroying all traffic in Anatolia, forbidding the revictualing of Constantinople, stopping ships filled with wheat, cutting off all routes leading to the capital by means of ditches and other works, intercepting all convoys of subsistence expedited by order of the basileis via beasts of burden, regular convoys, and extraordinary convoys.*

And that so very fatiguing and ruinous war, Skleros, after having inaugurated it in the summer of 987, far from discontinuing it after a small amount of time, pursued it for years. Such was the extraordinary influence that he exercised over his supporters, who remained passionately attached to him through his bloody peripeteias. There were never any desertions among them, despite what one might imagine could lead to that result, he knew marvelously how to seduce them by his rough and active kindness, to retain them by his largess, to maintain them all in perfect harmony, living with them in comradery, eating his meals with them, drinking from the same glass, able to call each man by his name, speaking with them only with benevolence.

Attacked in the west by the Bulgars who had just taken Berrhœa, a faubourg of Thessalonica, and in the north by Vladimir who had just seized Cherson, in reprisal for the delay of his fiancée, the Macedonian dynasty's distress became inexpressible. At whatever price, he needed to put an end to Skleros. "Stop shedding Christian blood," ordered the Emperor to his old lieutenant, through the mouths of his envoys, "return to reason, accept me for your lord and master designated by the Almighty." The hour arrived when the discouraged pretender, anxious for the future, feeling old age begin to assault him, stopped resisting his messages. He then obtained a complete grace for himself and his adherents. Formally renouncing the title of basileus, he was then accorded in compensation by the Emperor the infinitely esteemed dignity of Curopalate. There was a solemn and dramatic interview, if however the word interview is appropriate here. The old Skleros became blind suddenly.

Basil, from the top of his imperial throne saw coming toward him, walking, bent over with age, very tall, very stout, heavy and infirm, that extraordinary man who, for so many years, had shaken, like an earthquake, Constantinople and all the Empire. "There he is then," he said, "he whom I have so greatly feared! he comes to me like a supplicant, someone leading him by the hand." Rising before the old man who was kissing the ground, he extended his hand to him and began to chat with him. "Skleros," said Psellus, "pleaded the cause for his long rebellion, explained the motives for it, and why also he had given his submission. Basil listened to him with a sort of deference, ascribing to divine will that long succession of events and calamities.

The Basileus asked his interlocutor his advice, as a great military leader, on the best mode of personal government, in particular on the means to avoid, in the future, new revolts by great feudatories like those who, for so long a time, had come to bloody the Asian themes. "Skleros' response," says Psellus, "was not that of a captain having top command over imperial armies, but that of a *Panurge* (πανουργία). He counseled Basil not to tolerate at any price functionaries who are too powerful in his Empire, not to permit any of his principle military chiefs to possess great riches, but instead to bear down on them all incessantly with the most arbitrary exactions... to forbid them thus from becoming powerful or dangerous; not to tolerate any feminine influence in the sacred Palace, not to show himself magnanimous with whomsoever it might be, above all not to communicate his plans except to the fewest number of men."

All Basil II's subsequent policies prove that his advice, of dubious morality, but of great practical utility, were not forgotten.

Bardas Skleros died soon after that reconciliation. Such is the story, summarized as best can be, of the two Bardas who appear, in my eyes, without analogue, for as long as men search for the way back to Paradise lost, while weeping and killing their brothers.

Basil II's effective reign had begun four years earlier. His first act of imperial energy, a sudden act, completely unexpected, had been to get rid of his Parakoimomenos.

> *When John Tzimiskes died, Basil, despite his natural gifts of beauty, his so lively intelligence, his active, energetic and courageous soul, was still not, it seems, according to Skylitzes, Cedrenus, Zonaras, but a whimsical and*

voluntary adolescent, violently taken up with pleasure, unremittingly as well as immorally, solely occupied by the culpable and disorderly distractions of his age. Nothing of what was to be the great basileus of his later years had been revealed yet. The chamberlain, that unscrupulous and ambitious man, according to the chroniclers at any rate, would have profited by that sad state of affairs to make him worse and to monopolize for a long time to come his all powerfulness... To assuage the thirst for power which devoured him, he would not have hesitated, his historians affirm, to attempt to corrupt Basil forever, "to enchain," Lebeau says naïvely, "that young lion with voluptuousness," to plunge him into all sorts of debauchery. Only later, at the breakout of the great Bulgar war, Basil II, as if suddenly illuminated as to the duties of a sovereign, would he reveal himself, casting his first minister to the side, who was disconcerted by that brusque awakening."

In an instant, the young sovereign, transformed, decided to remove all type of authority from the famous chamberlain, who was so powerful under four emperors. And he did it without any concerns, without the least consideration, cruelly, with brutal simplicity, to everyone's stupefaction. Instead of asking for his resignation, he chased him from the Palace, placing him under house arrest, with express forbiddance of exiting. Almost immediately, he sent him away by force and exiled him, deprived of his immense property, acquired over the tears and blood of a million poor people, inundated with ignominy. Incapable of consoling himself with such a fall, the desperate chamberlain did not take long to succumb.[19]

The new master was about twenty-eight years old. From the moment of his first imperial act, Byzantium would for the next forty years know nothing but the absolute autocracy exercised by the inflexible will of one of the most complete men it ever had. The vast extent of the Greek Empire, at that time, is an immense difficulty for the historian. If the tenebræ, which are already very dense resulting from documentary penury, were aggravated even more by the

[19]Original footnote: Upon saying which, Schlumberger, who appears decidedly to have a preference for contemporary Germany, interjects, soberly I admit, an extremely unfortunate assimilation. "What happened," he says, "between those two men is what we have seen happen, in our own days, during the course of an *otherwise* illustrious disgrace." OTHERWISE? And a little later he says "... That tragedy in the Palace which recalls rather closely another more recent tragedy, one wherein a man of State, all powerful for so long, was easily deposed and broken by a young, fiery emperor impatient to rule alone." *Durus est hic sermo*, it is said in the Gospel of Saint John. With great reservations, I might accept Bismarck as Basil's eunuch chamberlain, even though I have very little admiration for that Prussian whose brutish work is already dead and rotting. But Wilhelm II, the Ham Actor, compared to the Bulgar Slayer, that degenerate imbecile's mustaches seen in a flash of lightning in the ambiance of that septuagenarian and unvanquished Hannibal! It is enough to make a man bellow or roar, according to one's species.

interior obscurity of him who was bound to dissipate them, one no longer sees very clearly where the remedy might be found. Such is unfortunately the situation procured by Schlumberger when he speaks of the extreme Byzantine West, that is to say of the poor themes of Lombardy and that of the always sacrificed Calabria, always exposed to the most terrible violence by Germans or Saracens, while waiting for the adventurers from Normandy, continually avenged by one or the other of them. He is forced then to speak of the Popes whose supernatural or supra-historical office is incredibly hidden to him. He has that in common, alas! with almost all modern historians. That satisfies the institutes and the universitarian pedants, but that does not satisfy deep souls.

I recognize that it is difficult to shed light, even a little, on all those horrible affairs of the Guelphs and the Ghibellines, which were beginning then and which lasted for centuries, and I recognize also that Schlumberger is not taken with unraveling them. But all the same, his ignorance or his misunderstanding of the indisputable and constantly miraculous Primacy of the Vicar of Jesus Christ makes him too insufficient. Aside from several episodes that one could believe to be purely Greek, such as the Romanesque rescue of the Holy Roman Emperor Otto II after the disaster of Stilo; or the marriage, to Charlemagne's successor, of the porphyrogenita[20] Theophanu, daughter of the stunning and prostituted

---

[20]porphyrogenita: it is questionable whether Theophanu was born in the purple, given she was the niece of John Tzimiskes. It is also questionable whether her mother was a Basilissa.

Basilissa; or even the amphibious story of Saint Nil, half orthodox and half Latin; – one would be authorized to suppose that that lover of Byzantium has something against the rival house of Saxony and that the three Ottos disorient him, troubling his sight. Impossible to omit them, however. So, Guelph and Ghibelline at one and the same time, or rather neither, like a true Byzantine, he falls on the Popes forced thus to pay for both East and West simultaneously, as is proper for Vicars of the Redeemer.

His chapters on Italy are disappointing for amateurs of the historical scrupulousness ordinarily practiced by Gustave Schlumberger and primarily for those, much rarer, who know about the infinite, œcumenical primogeniture of the Popes, in penumbras or in bright light. Example:

> *With the unfortunate Otto II, who died without having been able to exact vengeance on the Saracens of Africa, the glory of the house of Saxony, the most powerful in the world at that period of time, vanished forever. The scepter of emperors fell to the hands of a child, the little Otto III, his only son. The Byzantines triumphed. If their little basileis had been able, materially, at that moment to take advantage of the great victory of Islam at Stilo and the death of Otto, the Emperor of the East would have perhaps succeeded reinstalling, for a long time hence, his*

exarchs in Ravenna, and the Popes of his choice *in Rome, as Gregorovius[21] so well put it.*

Schlumberger has read so much that he believes one *chooses* the Popes! He believes it so much that he dares to write that "the Popes did not enjoy the least freewill under the iron fist of transalpine emperors." He has even spoken, on page 204, of Benedict VI, *elected out of fear.* "The simple people," he says, "have always loved the supernatural." He has gone to such effort to skim over the details that reasonable people will do well to renounce trying to discover in that historian the most fugitive resemblance to evangelical doves. "[The city of] Rossano had alone escaped the disasters of Calabria due to the strength of its walls, *rather* than to the protection of the Panaghia."[22] Habitually he calls a Muhammadan who became a Christian a *renegade*, which implies in his thinking the inexistence of the Truth. That was the opinion of Pilate who saw IT face to face. He estimates that the Arabs showed more tolerance than Christians. Doubtless, because they were in error. Truth *cannot* be tolerant. But one would need to believe that it exists in the flesh and bone, and that one can crucify it. There would be no end to it if I cited everything. The story of Saint Nil from which he has drawn useful information is curious, written by a man who does not believe in the supernatural. With the

---

[21]Gregorovius: Ferdinand Gregorovius (AD 1821-1891), a German historian who specialized in medieval Rome.

[22]The Panaghia: a small Byzantine church in the city of Rossano.

best intentions in the world, thinking that he is prais-
ing him, he shows him often detestable. I want to
mention the episode, apocryphal surely, of his disci-
ple, Saint Stephano, insulted and thrashed by him,
from morning to evening, till death. I want to mention
above all the strange argumentation of that so-called
saint not wishing that anyone should ransom the captives: "If God did not see the good of sinners as a result of their suffering in captivities, he would not tolerate them. So one must not try to prevent them."

As much as I can, I recommend reading the
Epic to anyone who wants to become familiar with
Byzantium of the tenth century, but with this very for-
mal reservation in advance that the reader must renounce any hope of learning anything about religious
affairs. In this respect, Schlumberger appears to have
put into practice, scrupulously, what one might call
the professional secret of historians.

Basil II, the Bulgar Slayer

After Tzimiskes and the unprecedented disorder that was procured, for twenty years, by the two Bardas; after Basil II, legitimate heir of the Macedonian house and now a man, took forcible control of the supreme power so as to keep it in the crux of his hand, for two generations, without sharing it, – one has the impression of a vast Roman road, perfectly straight and lined by sepultures, going to the ends of the earth, as under Trajan.

Indeed, there has never been a prince who so configured after himself the time in which he lived, nor one who so captivated his contemporaries with a more grandiose heart. There has never been, like it or not, an emperor who gathered so many, and *for so long*, around him, to prop up his formidable throne. The examples too often referred to of Augustus or Louis XIV are of no value here. Those famous and so mediocre mendicants lived exclusively on alms, having nothing to offer their benefactors besides monarchic ingratitude. Basil II was alone and wanted to be alone until his death. His miserable brother Constantine VIII, seated beside him on the same ivory chair against a golden background, but uniquely absorbed in his pleasures, does not count for one single day. In the Greek sense, Basil was a monk of the almighty. He had neither a wife nor children; at least, it was not possible to discover any. And he always wanted the same thing, which is the greatest power in the world, which makes a man most resemble god. Intellectual culture was not favored by him; on the contrary, he despised it, discouraged it, mocked it, like Napoleon could have done. Yes, Napoleon. And it is remarkable that Basil's hatred for letters has been punished precisely by silence. With the exception of the famous Psellus, a writer of various disciplines, nicknamed the Voltaire of the eleventh century, who was not familiar with that frightening and anticipated multiple of Charles XII and who could only speak about him by second or third hand, it is too certain that historians or poets have infinitely failed the Bulgar Slayer and that nine-tenths of his prodigious wars will only become visible in the light of God. But I mentioned the superhuman Napoleon and something else would also need to be mentioned. Here it is, to justify the audacious comparison, quite an extraordinary page by Psellus:

> *One of Basil's particularities was to disregard the traditional custom observed since time immemorial of limiting to certain seasons the favorable times for waging war. Contemptuous of not setting out for war except in the middle of spring, so as to regain winter quarters by the end of summer, as had been constantly done before him by all other basileis, his predecessors,* he was in the habit of bending the seasons to the exigencies of the goal he was pursuing with his expeditions. *He put up with, without complaining, the most bone-chilling cold as with the most blistering heat. He was truly a*

man of iron. Never, even when dying of thirst, did one see him rush avidly toward the desired source. He always knew how to control himself. He possessed a broad and deep knowledge of military science, *being not only perfectly instructed on what was important for a leader to know, but he was also well informed as to the duties and functions of a subofficer, or even a simple soldier. He was admirably good at placing each person in the position best suited to him, to drawing the best out of everyone. That so perfect familiarity with the art of war was the double product of his immense readings and a sort of inborn knowledge that assisted him in never growing slack.* He loved to fight in battle formation. *Detesting however to leave the field to chance, preoccupied with assuring himself against the chance of fate, he was not above finding recourse in ruses, in ambushes, in all the artifices of war. His favorite principle of tactic was that of never* breaking the battle formation. *For him, that was the secret to victory, the supreme recipe that would make his legions forever invincible, inaccessible to rout. As soon as each soldier, each cohort, each battalion had taken up its battle position, he did not allow anyone to veer from it, were it even to rush head-long at the enemy, unless by absolute necessity, and he punished severely, by chasing him from the army instead of recompensing him, any audacious soldier who, impatient for the given command, would move forward on his own initiative toward the enemy and put it to flight. When that so inflexibly rigorous discipline made his soldiers murmur, he was in the habit of telling them, smiling, with the greatest out-ward appearance of calm, that* he saw no other means anymore for them as for himself – not to be compelled to wage war. *He had as it were a double nature which made him perfectly adapted to the work of arms and the occupations of peace. In other words,* he was more ingenious in war, more imperial in peace. *When some one of his subordinates had committed a grave error in the field, he knew how to hide his anger admirably, to harbor it in his heart as if under ashes, to be better able later, once returned to the sacred Palace, to chastise the guilty party with the most severe discipline. Even though he was by habit very strict, inaccessible to pity, he knew when he needed to be softer and to*

*pardon faults when he was made
aware of attenuating circumstances.
Once he had made a decision, a decision often very slowly deliberated, no
human force could make him change
his mind. His attitude never changed
with respect to those whom he liked,
unless that was their fault. He always
made up his own mind, as if led by a
superior strength.* [23]

We are in the year 989, a terrifying year. Enu-
meration by Schlumberger: War against Bardas Phocas, war against Bardas Skleros, war against the Russians who take Cherson, war against the Bulgars who
take Berœa, war against the Iberians, insurrections in
Antioch. To so many miseries are added celestial
calamities. Winter was atrocious. Ice covered all the
rivers, the lakes, the sea itself. The earthquake on October 25 was one of the worst on record according to
the Byzantine annals.

The first Bulgar campaign, commanded by the
Emperor in person, had been a disaster. Under pain of
death for all Europe, that ferocious nation had to be

[23]Original footnote: "You fear war for my days? It is in that way, in
the time of conspirations, that one wished to frighten me with
Georges: he was always after me, that miserable wretch must
have had a mark on me. Eh well! he would have killed my aide
de camp, rather: but to kill me, it was impossible to kill me! Had I
accomplished the will of destiny yet? I feel myself *pushed*
towards a goal that I know nothing about: when I have attained it,
an atom will suffice to knock me over. Until then, all human
efforts can do me no harm." Ségur, *Napoléon in 1812*, Book II,
chap. II.

subjugated. "When the Bulgars," an anonymous person recounts, "were made to rise up against the Roman people, they ravaged all Thessaly and the country around Dolopia, and caused infinite problems to the Basileus of Ausones, that is to say, to Basil. Tax proceeds could no longer be transported into the capital. No Greek could circulate or undertake any trip without exposing himself to murder or slavery. The Basileus then, after the terrible rout of the Battle of the Gates of Trajan and many other reverses, considering himself incapable of resisting anymore by the human means within his scope, sought other assistance, really the best, the most sovereign. It consisted in prayers to the saints, who raise their high and invisible arms."

And immediately, the tenebræ.

"Here, a painful admission becomes necessary," said our groaning author. "Everything about that second Bulgar campaign, which must have been terribly hard and bloody and which lasted, we know this only recently thanks to Yahia's Chronicle, a full four years during which the Basileus seems almost never to have left Bulgaria; about those four years of uninterrupted, fierce fighting, – we know nothing or almost nothing about them, scarcely a single event of war, an incident of attack or defense, scarcely the name of a battle or a city taken. The Byzantines

> *Skylitzes, Cedrenus, Zonaras are even more silent, if that is possible, than their predecessors; they have simply suppressed, or nearly, any mention of those four years of war."*

A bit of patience, my dear historian, in a few years from now you will know everything, and you will be surprised – if surprise is still possible for you – to have been unable to decipher that nearly overloaded palimpsest that was within you, for we are really the *resemblances* of God and everything that happens during the course of the centuries has left its imprint in us. Each man's last sigh is a violent wind that opens that book in which all is written.[24]

A little curious by nature but temporarily resigned to know nothing about those four mysterious years during which the Basileus and his army seem never to have quit Bulgaria, I hasten to come to the campaign of Syria, much more known. Basil had received serious news that made him fly immediately to the other extreme of his empire. One of his armies had been beaten, quasi exterminated, at the Battle of Orontes, on September 15, 994. Aleppo was about to be taken, Antioch was menaced even. "Run, Basileus," wrote the Emir of Aleppo to the sovereign

---

[24]Original footnote: this complaint is moreover excessive, and revelatory of a veritable concupiscence of historians, the second concupiscence, said Saint John. "I put forward a volume of more than 600 pages in which I have not written one hundred lines of *hors-d'œuvre*." Thus writes Gustave Schlumberger in the Introduction to the *Bulgar Slayer*. Isn't that marvelous; what then does he dare to complain about?

of Rum, "hurry. We do not ask you to make war against the Bangoutekin and against the Egyptian troops. We beg you only to instill fear in them by coming to our rescue. The mere mention of your approach will force them to lift their siege. Know that if our city succumbs, the same will happen to Antioch almost immediately. Once Antioch is beaten, Constantinople will be in grave danger."

> *Basil, the consummate captain, as soon he was made aware of the extreme gravity of the situation, by a decision that seems to have been almost instantaneous, resolved, – in spite of his nearly indispensable presence in Bulgaria, in spite of the bad season that was beginning, which was, at that time of the year, an almost insurmountable obstacle to the progress of his troops, – he resolved to show up immediately in person at Aleppo, at the head of a relief army. Doubtless the emir's envoy had made it clear to him that there was not one day to lose, and that famine could from one moment to the next deliver Aleppo into Bangoutekin's soldiers' hands.*

> *So, abandoning momentarily to his lieutenants the effort of pursuing the Bulgar battle, the Basileus, collecting his forces from everywhere with a marvelous rapidity, "like a lion that*

pounces," left for the south in full winter with a powerful army. It was, in those days, a totally unheard-of enterprise to traverse thus, in a single bound, at the head of very numerous forces, in the middle of the bad season, spaces as vast that those separating Constantinople from upper Syria, for it is probable that the Basileus returned by relay from Bulgaria to Constantinople and that the campaign really set out from that latter city... Yes, it was a really prodigious enterprise and it seems, from the rare details that we have been given by the chroniclers, that Basil conducted it well, with hability, enthusiasm, mastery, a resolution worthy of the greatest captains. If we were a little less miserably informed, it is probable that the mad dash of the emperor Basil across the entirety of Asia Minor, from the shores of Marmara to the banks of the Orontes, in the winter of 994-5, in order to fly to the assistance of the emir of Aleppo, his vassal, would stand in comparison with the most celebrated military expeditions of antiquity and modern times.

... His need to hurry was at such a point, if he didn't want to arrive too late, that the expedition was trans-

formed subsequently into a rapid march of cavalry, like one of those gigantic raids that we have grown accustomed to recently in the American wars between the federalists and confederates... 40,000 troops would have taken more than three months to cross those spaces. Basil turned the difficulty around by an unusual measure which seems to have made a deep impression on the minds of contemporaries. He mounted his entire army... It is in this way that they crossed Asia Minor in sixteen days. That fantastic ride had its due reward. Basil reached Antioch unexpected, without anyone suspecting his arrival! Truth be told, of the 40,000 improvised cavalrymen that accompanied him at the start, no more than 17,000 were with him when he arrived, but many of those who remained behind had rallied incessantly. "That ride," exclaimed the Arab chronicler, "was something never before seen."

The terrifying news of the Basileus' arrival was like a lightning bolt to the Egyptian general. That great Basileus of Rum who had crossed an entire empire at a gallop, with his army, and who found himself only several hours' march away, when he was imagining

*him still deep in Bulgaria, frightened
him and put him immediately to flight.
Basil must have felt a deep feeling of
scorn on seeing the African army escape before him. But, all the same, the
goal of the expedition was fully attained.*

Such was the dazzling first Syrian campaign
by Basil II, who was depressed, three years later, by
the disaster of Apamea, cruel revenge by the Egyp-
tians on Basileus' lieutenant, Damien Dalasenos.
Aboulfaradj speaks of 10,000 Christian heads sent to
the Caliph. The captives, more miserable and perhaps
as many, were dragged to Cairo, sold in auction, and
led a horrible life of slaves for ten years after that, until a peace deal was struck...

When one reads the history of any people, the
Christian imagination is frightened to think of the almost infinite sufferings, the universal deluge of sufferings that hundreds of millions of men must have
endured, over the coarse of the centuries, in order to
complete "what was missing from Jesus Christ's Passion," according to the terrifyingly mysterious word
of Saint Paul to the Colossians!

The blow must have been rudely felt by the
Basileus and immediately determined his second
campaign in Asia, about which one knows, moreover,
very little; but from the time of his return from Aleppo, the war with the Bulgars appears to have been
more intense, more successful also and even to such a
point that one could have, it seems, foreseen already

the excessive humiliation of that hereditary enemy. The king Samuel was really the antagonist that the Bulgar Slayer needed. The war between those two leaders could not fail to be unforgiving. "The Bulgar monarch," says Skylitzes, "had a violent hatred for repose." And that's it; one must guess the rest. But at least one can assume the invincible obstinacy of a man who could resist for so long all the forces of such an empire and the warrior genius of such an emperor.

Schlumberger, who sees history primarily as a poet – by instinct or voluntary choice, from which his critical penetration is sometimes decoupled – has dreamt of the *superiority* of that barbarian.

> *Of course, he said, this must have been a man of first order, who knew how to grow his power so rapidly at the expense of his colossal neighbor, to the point of placing at peril the very existence of the latter; who knew how to turn undisciplined peasants and mountain people so quickly into regular armies capable of fighting successfully against the best troops in the world at that time and vanquishing them in pitched battle... He was a marvelous man of war, a man of iron, of perfect bravery, indefatigable, inaccessible as much to fear as to fatigue or discouragement, infinitely fertile in resources and in ruses in a difficult war, compared to others, a consum-*

mate tactician equal to the most able captains.

Eh, well! I disagree. That Samuel was, for me, simply a covetous and courageous brute, having almost nothing to lose and everything to gain, while commanding with an infernal authority, conceded by the demons of the Middle Ages, other brutes who were as rapacious and no less enraged than he. All his politic and all his strategy was to have his eyes constantly open onto the Greek world in order to profit at the very moment of difficulty or error, like famished wolves rushing at a traveler who stumbles. He was an enormous danger for the Empire, more pressing even than the Saracen peril, and I feel that Basil did not completely merit his terrible nickname, not having brought that danger to COMPLETE *extermination*, to irremediable depopulation.

Totally different was the situation of the Emperor of Byzantium, obliged to scrutinize the entire horizon, to divide his forces as well as his attention, and that gave him an apparent and, sometimes, dangerous inferiority. Samuel had need of perseverance alone, Basil had need of perseverance and genius. Under those conditions, the battle had to be long and in turn unequal. But what makes it appear so anguishing today, after so many centuries, is the *proximity*. The Greek Empire, in all its western part, could be compared to a giant with a panther on its back and forced, at the same time, to face many lions.

In 996, the Bulgar inundation was drowning Greece. An army corps would not have sufficed to protect a courier of the Basileus galloping towards Lacedaemonia.

> *The Bulgar tsar had, at the head of his armed bands, crossed the defile – so beautiful and so poetic, so joyful and so savage at one and the same time, – from Tempe in Thessaly between the gigantic masses of Olympus and Ossa, then traversed the majestic river of Pineios with its tranquil and slow flow, and finally branched out in every direction, burning, pillaging, and massacring, not only that beautiful province, but Boeotia, Attica even, penetrating even so far as the gates of the Peloponnese, across the isthmus of Corinth. All those unfortunate lands of Greece found themselves, once again, prey to the most atrocious ravages by that pitiless enemy. It was a nameless calamity. One has only to glance at a map to see what immense extents were covered by the Bulgar invasion's bloody wave.*

The Thessalonian garrison, lured into an ambush, had been, in large part, massacred. Basil, luckily, had a good lieutenant under his control, Nicephorus Ouranso, the great domestic of the West, raised in the art of war through the resentment of a long captivity. He needed Bulgaria, that one. He had orders to run straight at the invading army, and, of course, he had no need to be asked. He followed its tracks then, like a very sure hound, and finished by surprising it in the valley of Spercheios, farther than Pharsalus, farther than the wild chain of Othrys, at the foot of the gorges of meridional Thessaly. The Bulgar army was returning from the Peloponnese and from Attica, after an ample devastation, gorged on pillage, stuffed to the Adam's apple, swollen, stinking and pestilential, like a slaughterhouse fly. This was one of the bloodiest butcheries of a century where the slaughter was given for the asking. The Bulgars, unaware of the enemy's vicinity, or rather believing themselves protected by a river inundation, did not protect themselves. The Greeks found a ford and, in the middle of the night, descended on 30,000 or 40,000 sleeping men, whom they killed voluptuously. "Twenty years later, when the basileus Basil passed through those regions, going on a pilgrimage to Athens in order to thank the Very Holy Virgin there for the victories that she had accorded him, he contemplated the bones of the vanquished still strewn all over the gloomy plain which was white with their enormous piles."

> *Nicephorus Ouranos and his victorious army having despoiled their countless dead enemies, having freed the "Roman" prisoners that Samuel was leading behind him, and pillaged the enemy camp where he found an enormous booty brought back from Attica and the Peloponnese, happily retook the route to Salonica. Yahia says that the* magistros *reentered Con-*

*stantinople (probably in order to re-
ceive the honors of triumph), led in his
suite 12,000 Bulgar soldiers as prisoners. He brought with him also, a sinister baggage of 1,000 heads of the conquered, probably the heads of leaders
and officers. Of course, the 12,000
barbarian captives, in their ani-
mal-skin costumes, followed the generalissimo's triumphal procession on
foot, dusty and tired.*

*That terrible rout at the foot of
ancient Thermopylae, in the year of
the Lord 996, truly marks the turning
point of the intrepid Samuel's fortune.
One said correctly that that victory by
Ouranos, which definitively freed
Greece proper and the Peloponnese
from the incessant Bulgar menace,
constitutes one of the most notable
events in the history of the Greek
people, and that Basil II's valorous
lieutenant can justly pass for one of
the saviors of Hellenism.*

Unfortunately, the two most beautiful prizes,
the Bulgar Tsar and his son Romanos, although seriously wounded, had succeeded in escaping. The terrible war was to last another twenty years.

The details are so little known that one must
go right away to the most interesting places. Schlumberger's methodical work, a masterwork of patient re-

constitution, is not bound to be repeated. Here then is, in order to encourage the reader, the enormously frightening adventure of the 15,000 blindmen. That thing happened immediately after another great victory. We'll let our historian speak:

> Basil resolved to strike a terrible blow in order to terrify his stubborn adversaries and to bring the resistance to an end as quickly as possible. At the taking of the defiles of Cimbalongou, more than 15,000 Bulgar combatants had been captured alive by his soldiers. The Byzantine chroniclers affirm that he had all those captives blinded and sent back thus mutilated to their compatriots to serve as an example. By way of unprecedented refinement, for every one hundred blindmen they left one man with one eye, responsible for leading his companions. Then the Basileus sent this gruesome embassy back to the tsar Samuel. How many of those miserable wretches succumbed along the way? How many arrived at Prilopon? No chronicler has bothered to tell us. Only Skylitzes and Cedrenus relate that Samuel, already gravely ill, vanquished physically by his country's disaster, could not support the sight of even one of those columns of miserable wretches, moaning and staggering with each

*step. That too cruel emotion brought
on an attack of apoplexy, a rupture of
his heart or some blood vessels. The
unfortunate Tsar fell to the ground,
inanimate, dying. A strong medicine
brought him back to life for several in-
stants. He asked to drink some ice water and immediately fell down again in
a syncope from which he did not
emerge. He expired two days later. It
was really for grief on account of the
ills brought on his country, horror at
the sight of his mutilated subjects, with
their bloody orbits, who had been
right to rely on that man of iron, the
most noble personification of the fight
for national independence that those
somber days of the tenth century had
seen.[25] His death, which had taken
place on October 24 of the year 1014,
marked the hour of his people's
agony.*

*We have difficulty imagining such hor-
rible circumstances, that frightening
scene of torture, those poor Bulgar
soldiers arriving bound by the thou-*

---

[25]Original footnote: Is it expedient to declare, yet again, that I am infinitely far from sharing Schlumberger's admiration (!) for that despicable pirate, for that filthy brigand worthy of all tortures, who would have destroyed Greece entirely, together with its precious humankind, if God had not expressly created a Basil to prevent him. Consequently, that emperor has won my most vivid sympathy, and I feel no sentimental need to disguise it.

sands in order to endure that vile pun-
ishment, that tempest of hurlings of
pain and grief, then those weeping
columns of bloody blindmen, holding
hands, tottering and leaning against
each other with each step, then that
last confrontation of the moribund
king with those miserable wretches,
his tragic death on seeing all those
mutilated men whom he had known,
several days before, as combatants
filled with valor, today poor invalids,
condemned to living a terrible life.

After that, it seems to me that that great man's character is sufficiently demonstrated. The wars of extermination which our sensibilities of so-called Christian eunuchs make appear unacceptable today, were, in the tenth century, exactly within the framework of that period and extremely plausible. A Byzantium of honey, without blindings, without eyes gouged out, without impalement, without skinnings alive, without disembowelments or burnings alive, without dismemberment or hacking to pieces, after ample lapidation of excrements by the multitude; that Byzantium there would be fastidious and disgusting, to say the least. When one really gets down to it, the story of the 15,000 blindmen feels like an act of mischief. How many other examples, under Basil II even! Encouraged by experience, he ended up blinding all the Bulgar prisoners' eyes.

In his first Syrian campaign, the army was

continually harassed by countless groups of Bedouin, confident of the impossibility of running into the more heavily-armed Greek cavalry. Basil, irritated, had a group of forty of those African Cossacks taken by surprise and sent back with both their hands chopped off. The Bedouins, terrified, no longer showed their faces.

There was also the universal torture of political transplantation, more universal and perhaps more redoubtable, of which here is one of the innumerable examples. Bulgaria, almost defeated, was at the end of that forty-year war.

> *Faithful to his constant practice, Basil, in order to make it impossible for a new rebellion to arise, had all the valid population of Moglenes who were capable of bearing arms transported into Asia, to the other extreme of the Empire, "on the frontier with Persia," into his new possessions of Aspracania, today known as Vaspurakan. What an awful exodus for those free children from the mountains of Rhodope, so tenderly attached to their natal valleys! The miserable remainder of those unfortunates was, on the Basileus' pitiless command, despoiled of everything... Of course, here as elsewhere, Basil replaced the deported population by new colonists come from Asia, Armenians or Georgians*

> *probably. Those immense crisscross-*
> *ings of peoples incessantly covered the*
> *imperial roads by long theories[26] of*
> *unfortunate travelers. This explains in*
> *part the immense mix of Eastern*
> *races.*

Basil, however, was something more than a man of war. That emperor's hatred for the great proprietors is a paradisiacal refreshment. In his travels across the Empire, he had received infinite and identical complaints exposing that the poor peoples' possessions were found to be constantly grabbed or destroyed by the powerful, in consequence of that generous idea, common to all rich people in the world, that the possession of those stolen goods would rest secure with them, provided they had succeeded by ruse, gifts, or violence to prevent the dispossessed from filing a regular complaint before a prescribed period of time passed. Basil considered that oligarchy of more or less illustrious robbers like another Bulgaria that he had to wage war against. Schlumberger cites some examples of his imperial and very rigorous will to protect the poorest efficaciously, or at least avenge them, by punishing the acquirers of stolen property. He decided that "any benefit arising out of that prescription, whether its was forty years, or more even, would not be enforceable in order to maintain, neither in the present nor in the future, the manifestly unjust acquisitions. On the contrary, the original possessors, the peasants, who had formerly been chased

---

[26]theories: coming from the ancient Greek word meaning "embassies" or "solemn processions."

off their land by those proprietors of *latifundia* would
have the right to reclaim immediate reintegration of
their property, without being made to restitute the
purchase price received nor to pay any indemnity for
introduced ameliorations." One sees that this Basileus
had profited by the lessons of old Skleros. This is the
time when all the secular rancor of the Macedonian
dynasty bursts out in full vigor against those great noble clans of Anatolia, authors of so many terrible,
nearly-successful rebellions. Some, like the Phocas or
the Maleinos, had succeeded in detaining, for more
than a century, territories as vast as provinces, each
parcel of which represented an injustice.

Here is the most famous of those executions
of great landlords:

> *On return from the happy campaign in*
> *Iberia,[27] which had greatly enlarged*
> *the Empire, as the Emperor and army*
> *were crossing Cappadocia, the Byzan-*
> *tine annalists recount that the auto-*
> *crator received, in the vicinity of the*
> *stronghold of Charsianon, a splendid*
> *instance of hospitality in the domains*
> *member of the* magistros *Eustathios*
> *Maleinos, of the great Cappadocian*
> *family of that name, allied to that of*
> *the Phocas, the same Eustathios*
> *Maleinos who, in 987, had lent his*
> *residence to other leaders of the army*
> *reunited in order to proclaim Bardas*

---

[27]Iberia: Caucasian Iberia.

Phocas emperor. That opulent and sumptuous archon, returned to grace after so long a period of time, not content with offering hospitality merely to his prince, abundantly furnished victuals to his entire army. Also, Basil, under the pretext of showing him his gratitude for the splendid reception and in order to recompense him, brought that great landlord back with him to Constantinople. Then he kept him there for the rest of his life, never allowing him to return home, keeping him like a beast in a cage, defraying him generously for all his expenses in order to console him for the loss of liberty and natal land. Precursor to Fouquet[28] and so many others, that unfortunate Maleinos had, by the display of sumptuousness and provincial grandeur, excited the jealousy, and primarily the fear, of his sovereign. Of course, this latter suffered the consequences of defying those great provincial landlords of Asia... In order to cut short any new sedition done in imitation of Bardas Skleros or Bardas Phocas, Basil decided to make an example

---

[28]Fouquet: Nicolas Fouquet (AD 1615-1680), finance minister under King Louis XIV of France, who fell out of favor and was later imprisoned on charges of misappropriation of public funds. He spent the better part of the last two decades of his life in prison.

of Maleinos, who was wealthy enough to feed an entire army, and was thus recompensed for the brilliant reception he had given his sovereign, by loyalty or vanity... The Basileus, moreover, had need of money for his armies. He was not content with merely detaining Maleinos. On his death, he had all his property seized to the crown's profit. It was what John Tzimiskes had already proposed for the parakoimomenos Basil who, seeing himself threatened, took the first steps by having his sovereign poisoned. It is what the Basileus Basil did again later, under similar circumstances, never tolerating in his travels across the Empire that one of his great provincial landlords could become, by reason of wealth, a danger to the State.

In the same vein, there had never been anything more important than the reestablishment by Basil of the tax called *Allelengyon*, otherwise known as the *mutual guarantee*. That masterpiece of a duty had been invented at the beginning of the ninth century by Nicephorus the Greedy,[29] of astonishing memory, who thought of nothing better for a perfect emperor to do than to put all his subjects to the question until they had disgorged their last pieces of money. That "Equal of the Apostles," who spent all his time

---

[29]Nicephorus the Greedy: Nicephorus I (– AD 811).

amassing gold, as do American millionaires who are admired by a filthy people, and who hideously died on his riches, as they will do in turn; that eminent filth, that rheum of a potentate, clairvoyant by dint of cupidity, had very precisely discerned the proper fashion of dealing with the proprietors of it.

> *By that fiscal disposition, said Skylitzes, he had ordered at first that all those who could not pay the capitation tax should become soldiers, then as each of those obligatory soldiers would have for respondents his taxable neighbors, "the powerful," who would be bound not only to furnish to each of the said poor subjects of the Empire the arms necessary for their military service, as well as a personal bonus of eighteen gold coins each; but also to substitute for them for the payment, in their stead and place and in their name, of all usual taxes that those indigents could not settle. In a word, in each district, the richest citizens became the obligatory respondents for the poorest among them who found themselves in the impossibility of paying their taxes!*

I do not know why Schlumberger speaks indignantly about that just law, about that fiscal measure which he declares hateful, all the while stating that Basil was forced to recur to it in order to sustain the formidable battle on which the fate of the Empire depended. "It weighed terribly on the wealthy," he said, an occasion of ravishment for students of the Holy Spirit, which is all love and all justice! *Omnis dives, aut iniquus, aut hæres iniqui,*[30] said Saint Jerome.

> *That terribly vexatious law, whose precise text has not been preserved unfortunately, must have, fatally as well as rapidly, led to these two results: the ruin of the wealthy and an extreme animosity between the latter and the poor. On the other hand, it is necessary to say it, the Basileus not only procured for himself in that way resources in money and in men sufficient to the accomplishment of his grand designs, but he was assured also, to the detriment of a certain number of large landowners, of an unprecedented popularity on the part of the immense crowds of poor people and those dying of famine, who, until then, had been instead very hostile to him on account of the implacable durity of his administration and the unbearable taxes necessitated by a state at constant war. To be honest, he attracted to himself by the same act the hatred of the powerful, but he could*

---

[30]*Omnis dives...*: Latin for "Every rich person is iniquitous, or the heir to an iniquitous person."

*endure that better. His politics were
quite simple. As soon as the latter
showed signs of refusing to pay the* Allelengyon, *he would only have to raise
a finger to rouse the innumerable
masses of poor people who gained every advantage in the maintenance of
that Draconian administration.*

One may be wondering what Italy was doing
at this time. Exactly what father Hugo's King Sennacherib was doing. – King Sennacherib does nothing
for he is dead.[31] – Italy was dead and milling about,
like a huge cadaver devoured by vermin, such as one
sees it still and above all today. So dead that even
those among the Popes who were saints – and there
were many more of them than Schlumberger thinks –
could not resuscitate it.

The Rome of the One God, the Rome of the
poor, of the apostles, and of the martyrs seems to
have been struck dead on leaving the catacombs.
Something infinitely precious which nothing replaced
disappeared then, and the great doctors of the church
who came later did not shed as much light on it as the
living flames illuminated in the gardens of Nero did.
*Ut cum defecisset dies, in usum nocturni luminis ure-
rentur*, said Tacitus, who did not really know what he
was saying. The glorious house of Saxony, flower of
the Holy Roman Empire, had appeared at that moment to amalgamate that rotten nation. In reality, the

---

[31]The King Sennacherib...: a quote from Victor Hugo's *La
Légende des siècles*.

three Ottos thought they were drowning their almight-iness in the mud. The last of those amiable emperors of the West, Otto III, was on the verge of marrying the porphyrogenita Zoe, Basil's niece and first cousin, *filia ultra omnes virgines splendidissima*, just as her father had married the porphyrogenita Theophanu. The fiancée, in transit to her future spouse, had just disembarked at Bari, bearing the richest and rarest of gifts, when she received the unexpected, terrifying news of Otto's death...

With that pious and chivalrous emperor the greatest of dreams ended: the reconstitution of the West, not of the Empire of Charlemagne, but of the pure Roman Empire surrounded by all the Byzantine splendor. He wanted to make Rome the capital of the world, to restitute to the Queen City all its ancient magnificence, then when it was truly the *Domina mundi*.[32] His seal bore a representation of Rome armed with this legend: "*Renovatio Imperii Romani*." The Pope Silvester II, the illustrious Auvergnat Ger-bert, excited him in that pursuit. The news of his death at just twenty-two years of age, while it dis-tressed his fiancée, shook the world, moved every heart. One foresaw the atrocious fratricidal battles that it was going to trigger for the entire Empire of the West, for Italy above all whose history is as im-possible to learn as it is to tell represents, during all the Middle Ages which lasted one thousand years, the very chaos of hell.

The crowned hero's body was, in ac-

---

[32]*Domina mundi*: Latin for "master of the world."

cordance with his last request, piously borne across seditious Italy, his brave Teutonic warriors turning their collective bodies into a rampart around this coffin, over the glacial Alps and into the imperial city, Aix-la-Chapelle, in the old land of Germany, where he was buried on Easter Sunday, April 5. His remains did not sleep at all, like that of his father, in that Italy which was so hard, so disastrous to the Ottonides. Pope Silvester, not long afterwards, followed his beloved emperor to the grave. One may still see in the august subterranean tunnels of the "Vatican Grottoes," the fantastical asylum of so many great memories, the inscription of his tomb, unique debris of that vanished monument.

The Normans were not very far off anymore. Another two generations and the Greek domination in Italy will have been finished for good. Byzantine history was going to be lightened by the same measure. At the end of his long reign, the septuagenarian Basil, having crushed Bulgaria and dominated all the East, embarked finally on the realization of a project as old as his entire race: the submission of meridional Italy and the reconquest of Sicily, events that would have changed the face of the world. But it appears that God had had enough of all men's plans, and the quasi sudden death of that Slayer "sounded the death knell of Byzantine power on the peninsula."

Venice on the other hand, since the fall of Ravenna, was growing for the humiliation of Constantinople, but it was growing in the simulacrum of a very frightening respect.

> *There was, said Rambaud, a habit taken by the doges of the tenth century to send their sons on a trip to Byzantium; on their return, enriched by presents by the Emperor, decorated by the Protospathariat, they appeared to have more right to succeed their father; they had as if retempered their legitimacy in the eternal imperial legitimacy. The trip to Byzantium created even a sort of birthright among the sons of a doge; it was not the first-born who was the first to be associated with his father, but the one who was the first to have visited Byzantium.*

The Crusaders, vanquishers of Constantinople, in 1204, were led from Venice to the Golden Horn on Venetian vessels by the celebrated Dandolo. That irreparable doge, without whom the enterprise would have certainly aborted, was ninety years old. Like so many others before him, he had to *see Byzantium*, alas! In one place Schlumberger declares that the dismemberment of the Greek Empire during the Fourth Crusade was one of the great crimes in history[33] – an

---

[33]Original footnote: That, of course, by assuming the point of view of Christian politics *only*, without mention of the destruction of

assertion terribly verified by Mohamet II, two and a half centuries later, for the shame and misfortune of all the West. Such was the work of Venice. The sad Latin emperors, put on the thrown by Venice and who did not last sixty years, had left to the Palaiologos a fantastical Byzantium nearly without territory, reduced to the scope of its old orthodox walls, no longer protected by God, which the Ottomans had little trouble pulling down to the ground for all eternity.

It would not be fair to dismiss the phantom of the Bulgar Slayer without saying something about his last expedition into Armenia and Georgia, not long before his death, in order to chastise his vassal, the king of Georgia, Georges or Georgi I, Bagrationi sovereign of the Abkhazians, who was unjustly holding on to a part of Basil's territories. This Georgi had a redoubtable army, and the expedition nearly foundered. The Greeks, finding themselves in danger on several occasions, thought they were going to die for the cold in the Caucasus. But Basil's soul was infinite. The almost nonexistent documents permit us to see only the imperial army in retreat, defending itself poorly in the middle of the snow against the aggression of fierce peoples and obstinate plunderers in its

---

works of art by the Crusaders, which was the most complete and most *irreparable* destruction ever, whether one goes back to Alaric's Visigoths, or one goes only as far back as the Huguenots of Coligny, whose brigandage, for ten years, seems to have defied all comparison in the past as well as in the future. It was right and proper – one may say it in passing – that the Genoese and Anglican millionaires, naturally admirers of that brute, gratified us with his statue, ironically erected by subscription *in the neighborhood of the Louvre*.

pursuit. One thinks of 1812. It was a question, in both
cases, of putting an end to the world's vanquisher.
Luckier than Napoleon, the old autocrator could return home with his veterans and celebrate a triumph,
one last time, in Constantinople. Truth be told, in that
last expedition, as in all the others, the horror super-
abounds. Once again, we will let our historian speak.

> *The Byzantine soldiers had, by order
> of the Emperor who hoped in this way
> to put an end to his stubborn adver-
> sary, proceeded to the systematic de-
> struction of all the territories occupied
> by the king of Abkhazia. Divided into
> detachments, they spread out in every
> direction over those unfortunate coun-
> tries, with the rigorous injunction to
> massacre everyone, "sparing no one,
> neither old men, nor adolescents, nor
> children, nor young men, nor man, nor
> woman, nor absolutely any human be-
> ing of whatever age." Anything that
> would escape death was to be at mini-
> mum led into captivity. All the coun-
> tryside was to be ravaged, burned.
> Such was the terrifying custom of
> those eastern wars. The Byzantine
> army thus destroyed 12 districts en-
> tirely, according to Arisdagues, 24 ac-
> cording to Samuel d'Ani, in a word ev-
> ery portion of the kingdom of Abk-
> hazia, located south of the Kour, that
> is to say all of Georgia "save the por-*

tion situated beyond the uncrossable river," in other words the Kour. That pitiless destruction struck terror into the rural populations who, after many years, were enjoying a relatively substantial peace. Of these excesses of a brutal soldiery, Arisdagues has left us this striking depiction in spite of evident[34] exaggerations. "The Byzantines," he exclaimed, "gouged the eyes out of an infinite number of people (two hundred thousand! Yahia is not afraid to say). The noble ladies who were dragged across public places, their veil removed from their head, were exposed, in shameful nakedness, to the sun. Those who, previously, could barely find enough strength to visit on foot the suffering or the holy places of pilgrimage, today with their head and feet bare, walked before their insolent vanquishers, deprived of their adornments, dishonored, exposed to a thousand sorts of outrage. Small children were massacred everywhere. Each day, that terrible emperor raised his hand to add new evils to those who were overwhelming those unfortunate populations. Those formerly prosperous countries, thus depopulated, remained

---

[34]Original footnote: "Probable" would suffice.

ruined and deserted!" The chronicler adds this detail, hardly designed to surprise us, that the Russian soldiers of the imperial army would show themselves to be of an extraordinary ferocity in that execution. All other foreign mercenaries acted similarly. Sempad the Constable says that that methodical devastation of unfortunate Georgia lasted three entire months!

There were also "heaps, piles of human heads along the route, in order to strike fear in those who saw them," says the Armenian chronicler. But isn't it always the same thing since the Pentateuch?

Never, for centuries, since the great period of Justinian, since the glorious times of Heraclius, the Eastern Empire had never seen itself so powerful, so completely victorious. The Basileus reigned without contestation from the Danube to the extremities of the Pelo- ponnese. In Asia, from distant Colchis, from the frontiers of Armenia to those of upper Syria, all the populations docilely obeyed their lieutenants. In Italy even, things, in appearance at least, went even better, by the grace of the energy of the Catephanos. *The im- perial fleet was the first in the world at that time, the best commanded, the most ably directed and equipped. The*

*army was admirable and had shown,
during that long reign, what an energetic leader could demand of it, how
he could at will throw it alternately on
to the banks of the Danube, into the
mountains of Albania, into the valleys
of the Caucasus, on to the burning
sands of Mesopotamia or on to the
dazzling banks of Phoenicia.*

Now, as I have already said, God no longer
wanted that bloody mime, he had need of others, all
covered in blood as well, but not risking to awe, in order to prepare for the extreme abasement and destruction of that empire that had so greatly disobeyed the
Vicar of Jesus Christ! Basil, taken by a sudden illness, died on December 15, in the year 1025. He was
sixty-eight years old. He had reigned alone, "autocrat-
ically," following Yahia's expression, for nearly fifty
years. His reign was the longest in all the Eastern Empire, one of the longest in history. The patriarch
brought to him, at the last hour, the very holy Head of
the Precursor, piously conserved in the church of
Saint John the Baptist of Hebdomon, distinguished
relic which was later transferred, after 1204, into the
Cathedral of Amiens, where it remained until the
French Revolution. What has become of it since then?
Was the soul of the poor Slayer consoled? God only
knows, but the man in his agony wanted, before dying, the imperial crown placed on the head of his
brother Constantine VIII, already emperor and already himself an old man. A worse choice was not
possible.

"I am accustomed," wrote Psellus, "to attribute all the events of this world to divine Wisdom."

It is for that reason, very assuredly, that they are incomprehensible. It is beyond doubt that human wisdom is singularly disconcerted by the characteristic, manifest, constitutive and capitular powerlessness of the majority of great men to found something, no matter what, that is able to last more than one day.

To be honest, there have been rare saints who founded Orders that are still followed, more or less, several centuries after their death. The other lions, having become old, have scarcely the permission to die in peace, under the feet of asses.

One can also cite several famous heresiarchs who obtained, by privilege and diabolical predilection, permission not to die entirely. It is certain that Wilhelm II, who is not a lion, nor the son of a lion crossbred with a jackal even, obeyed, each day, in a very gentle manner, Luther, interred in 1546. and that his brother Nicholas[35] would have balked in horror at the dusty bones of that Cerulairian scoundrel, forgotten by the holy Angels for nine hundred years.

But in a general way, one can say that History is, *in appearance*, a continual reiteration of abortions. From Hannibal to Napoleon, nothing succeeds, in the final analysis, for any great man, and the most eloquent of poems, the tenth satire by Juvenal, itself become a commonplace, has no other object. There is hardly anything but the bourgeois who succeed in

---

[35]Nicholas: Nicholas II of Russia.

prolonging themselves a bit in their tadpoles, and still that ends finally in the penal colony or fraudulent bankruptcy by the second or third generation.

But to return to the Psellus' "divine Wisdom," it is doubtless indispensable to go further than that rhetor did and to accord an œcumenical prescience which he seems not to have had the least idea of. It is proven that God has no need of anyone's "day after," and that his eternal *today* satisfies him. Pettiness is no less asked for than Greatness in the laboratory of prodigies. Disparate or desperate successions operate inexpressibly in a mysterious and adored way, in view of compensations or ineffable recuperations. So it is very simple that a series of mediocre or abject emperors should succeed a personage like the great Basil in order to destroy his work. Thirty years after his death, in 1055, his empire was ruined forever.

Among those who will read these lines with more or less benevolence, is it possible to find an individual capable of sensing the strange difficulty, for a conscientious historian, of deliberately making a tabula rasa of a *future in arrears* for hundreds of year, to suppose, by a recoil of the mind, the inexistence of very great historical facts like the Crusades without whose notion it seems we could not even think about them? How to conceive of an epoch or, rather, how to put oneself in the shoes of a people of an epoch in which the Crusades had not even happened?

History, phenomenon or illusion – of all things the most incomprehensible, – is the unraveling of the web of eternity under temporal or transitory eyes. We think we see enormous spaces, we see instead but three paces ahead of us. My friend, my brother, turns the corner of the street. I no longer see him but in my memory, which is as moving and as deep as the sea. I am also as separated from him as by death. He is forever, well do I know, in God's eye, but for me he has dropped into a gulf. That corner of the street, it is any turning point in History.

There is also the anguish of magnanimous hearts. Son of Adam, our solidarity is infinite. Similarly, we have all sinned under the first Disobedience, we continue to sin *without excuse* in all the continuers of the Prevarication. So that in this admirably universal commerce, there is not one iniquity that we are not both the creditors and the debtors of. *Dimitte nobis debita nostra sicut et nos dimittimus debitoribus nostris*.[36]

All human atrocities, since the beginning, as well as the most holy acts, are imputed with justice to that newborn who weeps while sleeping in his cradle. The posterity of ten centuries, any more than the immensity of spaces, would not know how to constitute an alibi for immortals and for the sons of God.

History is for me like a ruin where I would have lived a most intense life before it became a ruin. Dolorous and paradisiacal feeling to have put one's heart into very ancient things that appear no longer to exist.

---

[36]*Dimitte*...: Latin for "Forgive us our debts as we forgive our debtors," from the Lord's Prayer.

I visit Byzantium like Schlumberger visited the ruins of Ani, ancient capital of the kings of Armenia, while holding up with my feeble hands, above that great vestige of my soul, all the starry firmament.

The Porphyrogenita Zoe and Theodora

And now we are going to gallop thirty years ahead to the stables of the Late Roman Empire. I have said it before, when beginning this work, immediately after the Bulgar Slayer, the Byzantine Epic is closed and the history of the Late Roman Empire becomes a horror. From Basil II to the first Komnenian, it is a scramble, a confused mass of eight emperors or empresses, and two tyrants or *apostates*, as they were called, two rebels dressed in the purple with an accompaniment of followers to make the Autocrator tremble; astonishing fury of love by the old Porphyrogenita Zoe; immense scandal in the elevation to the throne of the two Michaels and their terrifying end; a half dozen extraordinary massacres each amounting to 50,000 deaths possibly, without prejudice to the banal murders with which the history of Byzantium is continually ornamented for ten centuries; pestilences, famines, devastations, earthquakes, incredible cold waves, torrential rains, epidemics, and mortal schisms. There was never a more cursed epoch.

It is no longer any question of an "Epic" or Heroism, unless in reference to an individual and parsimoniously rewarded as appropriate. Everything is finished. Byzantium dies, Byzantium is dead. One might say that that poor old empire cannot get recover from the successor to its last great man.

"Constantine VIII," says Zonaras, "had a real predilection for gouging or plucking out eyes. He made continual use of that terrible punishment during his reign in order to reduce a crowd of eminent men to nothing." When the Barbarians or the Saracens ravaged a province, a very frequent occurrence immediately after Basil's death, quick! he had such and such a chief who was suspected capable of defending it and *from there* aspiring to the throne – blinded. That old imbecile, whose entire life had been a carnival, "died," says Psellus in his turn, "after having rolled the dice each day for his empire," between the intervals of punishment. Three years of that sort of shame were all the more irremediable when, deprived of male heirs, he wanted, after his death, to appoint a son-in-law who resembled him.

The recipe is precious, utilizable only, it is true, by the sole masters of the world. He had two old daughters, Zoe and Theodora, last branches of the Macedonian oak. The patrician Romanos Argyros was chosen as the spouse for the charming Zoe who was but fifty years old and had a future ahead of her still as one of the most illustrious actresses in history.

Romanos was married and, it was said, loved his wife, but heroism had stopped being compatible with the profession of Byzantium citizen and above all with friendship to the Basileus. As he appeared to weigh his options: "I leave you the choice," said the ferocious moribund Constantine, "either have your eyes gouged out or accept my daughter's hand in marriage and the Empire." Naturally, Argyros chose emperor.

This new master lasted five and a half years. No less was needed for this other gaga to accelerate the putrefaction in a definitive manner. He is not reproached with cruelty, which is surprising, but with the vanity of Xerxes and a proconsul's rapacity. He believed himself called to the fulfillment of the conquest of Syria, flattering himself for a strategy superior to that of Nicephorus and Tzimiskes. He had a magnificent army, which he commanded in person, but which was horribly massacred, and owed the salvation of his miserable hide to the devotion of his Varangian guard.

Having returned pathetically to Constantinople, where one presumes he did not dare to triumph, he decided to renounce the glory of arms and apply himself to becoming a perfect man of Byzantine finances and a builder.

> *The great basileus Justinian had acquired immortal glory by constructing the temple of Divine Wisdom. Consequently, Romanos III decided to erect, he too, an admirable church under the vocable of the Mother of God. This was the famous church mentioned by Periblepte which no longer exists today, but which remained standing for nearly six centuries, among the most splendid gems of Byzantine architecture. Huge works. "An entire mountain was gutted," exclaimed Psellus*

with emphasis, "in order to furnish the stone needed for the walls. The art of extraction was found suddenly elevated to the height of a branch of philosophy and the workers employed in this work were gladly compared to those of Phidias, Polygnote, or Zeuxis!" That construction became the great, almost single affair of the Basileus. All those who did not show themselves to be fanatical about that pious construction were immediately classed among the Basileus' enemies. All those who, by courtliness, spoke about it with admiration, passed immediately into the rank of friends of the first degree. Nothing seemed beautiful enough, sumptuous enough for the dear edifice. The imperial treasury was completely tapped for it. The great flow of gold was diverted uniquely in that direction."

To that edifice, which devoured Romanos, was added a monastery for men, of extreme luxury, a famous monastery where it was the custom of emperors to celebrate the remarkable feast of the Presentation.

Unfortunately for Romanos, none of his Byzantine subjects was as harshly *imposed* on as the luxurious Empress to whom it was forbidden to have access to the imperial Treasury and who had to be contented with a strictly limited annual pension. It was the main motive for the death of that basileus. The old Basilissa, enraged moreover by lust and abandoned by her impotent spouse, became passionately amorous with one very handsome young man from Paphlagonia, – *flos Asiæ*,[37] as Juvenal said, – a counterfeiter by trade and brother of the eunuch Joannes, the grand chamberlain, to the point of loving him publicly and, so to speak, under the very eyes of the Emperor who was nowise troubled: "I heard it affirmed," says Psellus, "that the basileus Romanos feigned ignorance about the liaison of the Basilissa with Michael, but in reality he was perfectly up to speed on that mad passion. Only, as he knew very well the temperament of the Basilissa, he affected to see absolutely nothing, preferring that Zoe had but her one lover, desiring moreover that his old spouse abandon herself in total tranquility to her illicit love affair."

The denouement was this. That complaisant husband, having become suddenly very ill, poisoned very probably, but not dying so quickly, was drowned in his bath and the lover, now spouse and emperor, began to reign under the name of Michael IV, the Paphlagonian. This return of the name Michael in such circumstances, 167 years after the death of Michael III, assassinated by the first Basil, founder of the House of Macedonia, must have sounded the death knell of that dynasty for some people.

The story of Michael IV's enthronement is of

---

[37] *flos Asiæ*: Latin for "flower of Asia."

an adorable simplicity. It had to do with an extreme
promptitude. It was a matter of life for the two lovers,
and for several others. The eunuch Joannes, the great
machinator, did not lose an instant.

> *The patriarch, summoned immediate-*
> *ly, found Michael waiting for him in*
> *the golden lamé robe, seated with his*
> *imperial fiancée on the throne of*
> *basileis. She herself, by her own*
> *hands, had already placed the diadem*
> *of Constantine's successors on her*
> *lover's head, before taking her place*
> *beside him in the unmoving and hier-*
> *atic attitude consecrated over the cen-*
> *turies. At the same time, Palace em-*
> *ployees charged with mortuary cere-*
> *monies were busy with funeral prepa-*
> *rations and the toilette of the unfortu-*
> *nate Romanos' cadaver.*
>
> *Addressing himself to the old, fright-*
> *ened patriarch, Zoe, showing him her*
> *new master, that adolescent with rosy*
> *cheeks, ordered him to unite them in*
> *wedlock, then and there. As for him-*
> *self, terribly troubled, trembling with*
> *fear, hesitating all the same before the*
> *enormity of the crime, muttered some*
> *unintelligible words. Psellus says that*
> *he didn't even manage to let out a*
> *sound. But the eunuch Joannes pos-*
> *sessed an admirable knowledge of*

men. On his advice, Zoe immediately placed into the timid prelate's hands the enormous sum of fifty livres of gold, and an equivalent amount for his clergy. "That liberality," says the excellent Lebeau, "fixed the incertitude of the prelate." The old man, having been convinced, seemed to return to his senses. He immediately went about what was demanded of him, married the two murderers, so fantastically disproportionate in terms of situation and age, summoning the divine benediction over them, and finally crowned the adventurer from Paphlagonia, the old counterfeiter, brother to the eunuch. He made that man of nothing into a Roman basileus, the highest dignity in the world at that time, on a par with the Pope and the German Emperor. Only in Constantinople could such an extraordinary thing come to pass: an adolescent of obscure birth, only yesterday an unknown person, today seated on the secular throne of the basileis-successors of Constantine, representing God on earth, having become the absolute master of half the known world, by the insane caprice of an old lover, heiress to the illustrious Macedonian dynasty!

Immediately afterwards, the great dignitaries,

old generals or magistrates, came to adore the newly
crowned ephebe who, perhaps, some months earlier,
had served them their dinner plates or washed their
feet. The City was indifferent.

That new basileus is one of the most discon-
certing historical figures. Epileptic already, and soon
struck with dropsy, he stopped functioning as a lover
and became an ascetic, a good emperor, a *hero* even.[38]
Despite his brother the eunuch Joannes, who was an
unsurpassable scoundrel, it happens that that adventurer Michael, having become so great, also wanted to
become a good man, and he wanted it so badly that he
went, as I have said, as far as heroism inclusively.

One imagines nothing more surprising and
more dolorously poignant than that reign of seven
years eight months. "Michael," says Psellus, in a sort
of funeral oration, "had done and meditated on great
things in his reign. Rarely did he not succeed in those
undertakings. In all impartiality, I am forced to admit
that the sum of his successes exceeded by far that of
his insuccesses, and I estimate that that man really
had a just end."

Ah! if he could have thrown his brothers over-
board, and if he had been less constantly, less mortal-
ly ill, he would perhaps have brought the Empire back

---

[38]Original footnote: On the occasion of asceticism, Schlumberger
evacuates, page 176, appreciations of an afflicting Protestantism,
going so far as to pride himself on, against what he calls
"religious monomania," his so-called quality of a "child of the
twentieth century," which he could have been the father of as
well as I. Displaced coquetry on the part of a member of the
Institute.

to the point of grandeur of the last years of the Bulgar Slayer! But what a force it would have taken! All was going badly, as if the effective master, the eunuch Joannes, a kind of monster, surprisingly referred to as "Orphanotrophos" – protector of assisted orphans, de-nomination which comes from one of his first respon-sibilities – as if he had been a veritable demon.[39]

The poor Basileus could have repented his crimes and inflicted on himself the harshest peni-tences, renouncing every earthly consolation, – it would not have done any good: his baneful brother

---

[39]Original footnote: The pious Skylitzes, who recounts the success of the eunuch's wickedness, cannot help adding these words: "The events nevertheless bear witness that all this displeased God, for at the eleventh hour of the holy and great Easter Sunday, on April 14, two days nearly after the drama – a violent storm, accompanied by a terrible hail, destroyed trees, vineyards, and harvests. Houses, churches even, were knocked down by the tempest's violence. The disaster of the harvests was such that that year of 1034 was almost barren. And the following Sunday, April 21, towards the third hour of the night, a star, a flaming meteor appeared in the sky, projecting so vivid a light that it blotted out, by the force of its rays, all the other stars to the point that many believed that the sun had risen! And the unfortunate Basileus continued to be tormented by his so dreadfully dolorous malady. No divine or human aid came to wrest him from his frightening suffering." – "A star," said Aboul-faradj, "falling with the speed of a bolt of lightning, was followed by a pestilence that killed seventy thousand people in Bagdad." – Skylitzes recounts even, in the following year, that the locusts, coming alive again out of the sand banks of the Hellespont, infested again the Thracians' theme. After having effected thus their ravages for three years on all the banks of the strait and in that theme, they went to die in Pergamon.

I wish I could express my tender feelings for these journalists of the eleventh century.

made him commit, unbeknownst to himself, the worst injustices. It is in this way that Maniakes, the greatest warrior of that time, the victor of Syracuse, was arrested in full triumph, on the eve of reconquering all of Sicily, brought back to Constantinople, and thrown ignominiously into irons for having displeased a blackguard who was cherished by the powerful minister. Event, moreover, excessively banal in the history of Byzantium. How many other iniquities!

The times, what is more, were atrocious over and above what one said perhaps or thought even. It happened one day that Saracen pirates who devastated the Cyclades and the western themes of Asia, having been captured in great numbers, were impaled on stakes fixed at intervals along the coast ravaged by them, from Adramyttium to Strobilos, – or Termeron of Caria – about the distance from Lesbos to Rhodes, which must be about one hundred leagues.

There is also for the amateurs of anecdotes, the amiable original of the tale of *Ali Baba and the Forty Thieves.* It is worthwhile citing.

> *The city of Edessa had nearly been taken by the Saracens in a singular surprise move that Skylitzes and Tchamtchian recount, which this latter writer places in the year 1038. Twelve from among their chiefs came, one day, followed by 500 cavalrymen and as many camels, each loaded with two large boxes, a thousand boxes in all. They were, they said, gifts that their*

nation, of which they were merely the
envoys, addressed to the Basileus so
as to render him homage and make
him favorable. The governor gave, in
Edessa, the friendliest welcome to
these strange travelers. He invited the
chiefs to a feast, but he did not invite
their cavalrymen nor their camels into
the city. While those invited savages
banqueted at the expense of the
Basileus, an Armenian vagabond, who
understood Arabic, when to beg in the
Saracen camp. As he wandered between their camel-hide tents, he was
surprised to hear one of the boxes in
conversation with its neighbor and a
voice that rose asked: "Where are
we?" He ran to share his discovery
with the governor who, leaving his
guests at the table, galloped into the
enemy camp with an elite detachment.
The infidel cavalrymen had left the
camp to go foraging. The Byzantine
chief immediately had the boxes
opened. In each box an armed soldier
was found. Skylitzes says that there
were two soldiers to a box. They had
planned, thus, to take control of the
city at night. As they opened each box,
they killed the men who came out.
Also, as the dispersed cavalrymen returned to the camp they were dis-

*patched. Then the governor returned
to the chiefs whom he found feasting
still and already drunk. He had them
murdered as well, sparing only one
whom he sent back after having his
hands, nose, and ears cut off, in order
to give an account of the success of his
deputation to his compatriots.*

One can also mention the innocent mischief of
the young caliph of Egypt, Al-Zahir, assembling
2,660 young women in a mosque and having them
immured. They died of hunger and, for six months,
their bodies remained without burial. Never, it appears, had anyone danced or sang as under the reign
of that caliph. The stories are endless. But it seems to
me that those little stories are nothing compared to
this one:

In Armenia, a certain emir, long a prisoner of
the imperials and finally freed by the Seljuk victors,
in order to avenge the suffering of his captivity had a
pit dug as deep as a man is tall. He had it filled with
the blood of the prisoners whom he gave the order to
be massacred. Then he stepped into it and took a bath
"in order to drown the rage that was devouring his
heart."

And if all that was not enough, there was, in
order to replace the Face of God, the very young Pope
Benedict IX, shame of shames, "representing the
most frightful [person] of that frightful epoch."

In 1040, the poor Paphlagonian Michael IV,

fifty-fifth emperor since Constantine the Great, came
to the end of his miserable life.

All his thought was concentrated on
the proper means to inspire some pity
in his preferred patron, Saint
Demetrius, the great military saint,
protector of Salonica. He also habitu-
ally sojourned in that city and in the
very church of the megalomartyr, to-
day Kassimyeh Djami, where was
erected and still stands the tomb of
this latter, incessant object of an im-
mense and secular devotion... The
poor man almost never left the tomb of
the saint, the glorious callinique, as
the Byzantines loved to call him in
memory of the innumerable victories
that his intervention had brought to
the imperial armies over so many cen-
turies. Lying down beside the famous
tomb in the humid shadows of that old
church, that strange basileus spent
long nights there in ardent prayer, in
perpetual oraisons, seeking vainly for
the sleep that evaded him, supplicating
the saint in a loud voice to heal him.

What drama! Several years ago, I vis-
ited Salonica. I entered that venerable
mosque of Kassimyeh where Muslim
tolerance permits the orthodox faithful
to go and pray beside the tomb of that

great Saint Demetrius, whose splendid and famous church it was, ruined today, and to gather there the balm exuded by the holy body interred for many centuries. As I walked through that somber church, it seemed to me that I could see beside that sordid tomb, now devoid of its magnificent decorations, the imperial penitent of nearly nine centuries ago, the haggard Paphlagonian, trembling with fever, disfigured by his terrible illness, lying in the miserable rags of some ascetic, imploring with his very humble voice the pity of the holy warrior, imploring primarily pardon for his crime, and I said to myself stuporously that that pitiful supplicant thus prostrated was the Basileus of the East, Constantine's successor, the all-powerful master of half the world, the basileus Michael crowned by God, the equal of God on earth.

The eunuch, naturally, profited by that powerlessness. There was no dastardly action that he did not do in order to torment and overwhelm the Empire's subjects, according to the chroniclers. What follows is the unprecedented ending.

I do not know anything as extraordinary as the Bulgar campaign and the crushing of the Bulgars' redoubtable sedition by that moribund.

*At first news of that dangerous upris-
ing, Psellus and Zonaras recount,
Michael declared that at all costs he
would march at the head of his troops.
"It would be iniquitous," he repeated,
"that he who has not to date brought
any aggrandizement to the Empire
should, on the contrary, happen to
lose a parcel of it." In vain, he was
supplicated to renounce his plans.
That dolorous agitation augmented his
malady even more. It swelled prodigiously. Making up for his physical
weakness by his moral energy, he
made the last preparations himself. At
the head of the elite of his troops commanded by an elite of officers, he left
Salonica by an incredible effort of will
and marched straight to the Bulgars.*

*... Bulgaria was pacified, crushed
once again. In that year of 1041, we
do not know what date exactly, the
Constantinopolitan crowds acclaimed,
in the City protected by God, the triumphal entry of that victorious but dying basileus who wanted to die standing up. Michael the Paphlagonian
brought with him, behind his white
courser, a multitude of Bulgar prisoners, the most illustrious boliades.*

Psellus recounts that he saw with his

own eyes that extraordinary entry. He saw the unfortunate prince pass by on his horse. He looked like a cadaver. His disproportionately swollen hands had difficulty holding the reins. His features were disfigured by edema to such a point that he was unrecognizable. "In this way, he demonstrated to the Romans," exclaimed the rhetor, "that love of the fatherland can resuscitate the dead and that zeal for great actions can triumph over the most extreme physical debility." The poor failing sovereign was brought to the Palace.

On December 10, 1041, which was to be his last day, abandoning his apartments in the old Palace, Michael had himself transported back to his dear monastery of Saints-Anargyres which he had founded and asked, in order to die in peace, for the monastic habit... Usage and last recourse of emperors and great Byzantine criminals, for a thousand years. Soon, as it was time for the new religious to go pray and chant in the chapel of the convent with the monks his brothers, the poor man rose quietly from his bed, asking to put on the coarse sandals of his new state, but they were not yet ready. Disappointed by that delay, rather than put

> *on again the red* campagia *or purple*
> *boots, a symbol of what he had been*
> *on earth, the neophyte wanted to go*
> *barefoot to church. He went forward*
> *with difficulty, held up on both sides*
> *under the arms, breathing with diffi-*
> *culty, already almost in the agony of*
> *death. His strength having failed him,*
> *he had to regain his bed, having lost*
> *his voice and breath. He remained in-*
> *ert and silent for a while, then he gave*
> *up the ghost.*

Let's move on to Michael V, called the Kalaphates or Caulker because of his previous profession. No consolation to hope for from that man there. During the entirety of his reign, which lasted four months, the earth trembled, according to Skylitzes. His elevation was a dodge. Zoe, having become sexagenarian and a widow for the second time, was not thinking yet of a third marriage. The eunuch, determined to hold on to power and seeing the death of Michael coming, had imagined to have adopted by the Basilissa, legitimate heir of the house of Macedonia, an execrable scoundrel of the lowest level, his own nephew, whom he believed incapable of independence. He was immediately repaid for his clairvoyance and his kindness. One of the first acts by the new sovereign was the removal from office and ignominious exile of the Orphanotrophos. Nobody wept for that minister, execrated by all the Empire for his exactions. Instinctive hatred for the impost, banal key to all histories of revolution.

The harm, until then, was not great and the caulker could have held on. The people of Byzantium, already habituated to illicit emperors, would have put up with that ignominy. They would have pardoned him even for having emasculated almost everyone who was related to him by blood ties. "Many of them were married men, having beards on the chin, already even the respectable fathers of family!" Unfortunately for him he wanted also to get rid of his adoptive mother, the old Basilissa, colossal gaffe that un-leashed one of the most enormous popular furies ever seen. The event, which the great historian Psellus was ocular witness to, was documented in great detail. There are few events so tragic.

Everyone in the capital stormed the Palace in order to kill the Basileus and his most noble uncle Constantine who tried in vain to instill courage in that puny runt, reminding him of the famous words of Denys the Tyrant, "that a monarch, to descend from the throne, must be dragged by the feet."

In vain, those two men in despair showed the old Zoe, brought back in total haste, to the people. It was too late. They had already sought, in her cloister, her sister Theodora, the other Porphyrogenita, heiress herself as well to the crown of the great Basil, and they had proclaimed her loudly. For it was a rage for legitimacy that was motivating that multitude.

After a fierce battle of fifty or sixty hours which cost, it is said, the life of 3,000 citizens, the ri-oters won the day. The Basileus and his most noble uncle, dragged from the sanctuary where they had hoped to find refuge, submitted to their destiny. Theodora had given the order to gouge their eyes out. Such was the denouement of that appalling reign.

> *After the victims were brought to Sigma Square, irons were sharpened. "When the uncle and nephew saw that there was no more hope," says Psellus, "a part of the public being against them, the other part letting things follow their course, their souls were seized with fear, remaining speechless. A senator who happened to be there made an attempt by some good words to instill courage in them." Psellus who had followed the tumultuous cortege, was present at the end of the drama. The Basileus had an immensely pitiful attitude, moaning, lamenting, invoking all those who approached him, humbly supplicating God with his hands clapped together, extending them towards all the churches, towards all that he saw. Skylitzes says that he cravenly supplicated that they blind his uncle first, according to him, the only guilty one. The very noble uncle, on the contrary, after having, he also, shown some pusillanimity, completely regained his composure. With an otherwise virile soul, compared to his nephew, he seemed bravely to reconcile himself to the fate that awaited*

him. As the executioner drew near, he didn't resist. As the crowds, avid to see his punishment, suffocated him almost, not leaving any free room, he addressed the officer in command with a firm voice: "Push back the crowd," he told him, "and you will see that I submit to my fate with courage," then, as they were about to bind his hands, he refused, saying to the executioner: "If I budge, you will be free to tie me to the post." Then, he lay down on the ground, without turning pale, without a cry or a groan, immobile like a deadman. They gouged out his eyes while Michael gasped for breath in anguish, beat the air with his hands, tore at his face, lamented out loud, filled the air with his cries.

When the horrible mutilation was complete, the very noble uncle, rising from the ground, without anyone's assistance, showing everyone his empty orbits gushing blood, held up by several faithful, conversed with them with so surprising a calm, so superhuman a courage, that he seemed indifferent. Then it was the Basileus' turn. This latter displayed so great a despair, he addressed such crazy prayers to heaven that the executioner, afraid he would put up a struggle, had him bound tightly. Then it all was over!

Here I am now with almost no strength left to continue. Constantine IX the Monomachos is discouraging by far. I do not know even whether I would prefer him or not to the rascal just mentioned. The elegances of that great Byzantine lord make him seem more detestable to me.

It was Zoe and Theodora now, two old women who hated each other, on the throne. That soon appeared intolerable. An emperor was desired. Theodora obstinately rejected any matrimonial idea, having, moreover, for a long time, ceased to be marriageable, even for "black elephants." Her sister, although older, still had, it seems, a bit of ragout left in her. Psellus has returned multiple times to the portrait of that woman whose beauty was famous. "Considering only," he says, "the perfect harmony of all her person, anyone who didn't know her true age could have taken her for a young woman almost. Her skin had kept all its firmness; all was quite full and shiny with her; one saw neither a wrinkle nor an altered contour..." "She was the blonde sultana, with big eyes, and menacing eyebrows," adds M. Rambaud, "who had the Empire at her disposal."

In spite of her sixty-two years, one has to believe that she was not yet completely spent, for she had the hots, at least for the moment, for the handsome Monomachos whom the great ladies of Byzantium had a crush on. From the time of her first marriage, she was said to have greatly noticed that individual whom some already saw succeeding Romanos

III. Also, with the arrival of Michael IV, he was, under the pretext of a plot, interned on the island of Lesbos where he spent seven years. Such was Zoe's choice. Historians are unanimous in representing him as a player with character, eminently frivolous, who saw in the profession of emperor nothing more than a marvelous occasion to make whoopee. For twelve years, it was one revel after another, and that relatively long reign would be barely worth mentioning if one passes in silence over a man like Maniakes, already mentioned, and if it weren't for the immense catastrophe of the Keroularios schism.

What do we care about the ravishing Sklerena, devourer of the public Treasury, Pompadour or Dubarry of that anticipated Louis XV? What do Zoe's complacencies or tolerances for that left-handed basilissa matter, graciousness paid in the most ingenious and expensive of gifts that the favorite lavished her with? Zoe, grown calm over the years, no longer felt any pangs of jealousy. As for Theodora, no less adulated, she was much more removed to hold a grudge against the seductive creature.

Psellus is curious to consult with respect to that old Zoe, all whose acts can be summarized in three words: lust, perfumes, and piety, which give her more or less the character type of a woman of high society, bourgeoise or duchess, of the twentieth century. She had ended up transforming her bedroom into a laboratory of perfumery where women domestics gathered around a large fire, perpetually occupied in the crushing, grinding, or mixing of unguents, balms of all kinds... Everything of the sort that she fabricated, all her most precious recipes were moreover uniquely consecrated to the needs of religious service in the churches, for she was infinitely devout. As she did not occupy herself with anything else than that pious fabrication, the Basileus had all the leisure in the world to engage in his little love affairs. The Basilissa's *religion* suggested to Psellus several idiotic lines, which it is indispensable to cite: "She surpassed," he said, "in her love for God, all the women and all the men of her time." (It must not have been difficult, primarily in Byzantium.) "God repaid her for it by making her attain the sublimest regions of purest spiritual light." That affirmation will surprise only some Western sacristans. Assassination and adultery had prepared the basilissa so well!

I am impatient to get to Maniakes, an absolutely heroic soldier of fortune, who would have become emperor if anything of divine benediction had remained over that detestable empire. To mention merely one act of war, the conquest of the great city of Edessa by that sublime adventurer at the head of 400 men, followed by its victorious defense against all the Mussulman forces of Syria and Mesopotamia, boggle the imagination. That occurred under Romanos Argyros who had the goodness not to have his eyes gouged out. Under Michael IV, he was less fortunate. His magnificent successes in Sicily were repaid by disgrace and prison. Given his freedom by the Kalaphates[40] who had him named magistrate or

---

[40]Kalaphates: Michael V Kalaphates.

catepano of the Italian themes, – the furious fool re-
pairing, in this way, the atrocious injustice of a sage,
– then disgraced again by Monomachos, odiously and
imprudently maltreated in his properties, outraged in
the person of his wife, we are going to see him advance like a tempest over Constantinople. Historians
speak of the totally prodigious character of that pretender to the throne. We will cite Psellus again, constant witness of the most considerable events of that
epoch:

> *I have seen up close that man whose*
> *command had been revoked in so infa-*
> *mous a manner, and I have admired*
> *him. Nature had lavished on him all*
> *the gifts necessary for a military lead-*
> *er. He was ten feet tall. One needed to*
> *raise one's eyes from below in order*
> *to contemplate him, he was so tall. He*
> *had a terrible expression on his face,*
> *his look was frightening. When he*
> *spoke, it sounded like thunder clap-*
> *ping. His hands were made for throw-*
> *ing down walls. He had the impetuosi-*
> *ty of a lion. All the rest accordingly.*
> *His reputation surpassed reality even.*
> *There was not a single barbarian who*
> *did not tremble on hearing the name*
> *of that man, the ones for having seen*
> *him, the others for having heard speak*
> *of him...*

His reputation as a hero of immense bravery

was such that a crowd of people of all ages and all conditions came to ask to serve under him. Happily disembarked in Dyrrachium with his loyal and numerous troops, hoping to recruit others along the way, he began to march through savage Macedonia toward the capital of the world. That caused an immense stir in the Empire. Everywhere, people believed him basileus already. He didn't become one, because one does not know what God wants, and because the things that seem just and desirable in life almost never happen.

The tears that flowed because of that timeless disappointment could have carried all the ships of terrestrial Hope and Grief.

That Alexander, more fortunate moreover than the other, who had died in a bourgeois bed in Babylon, perished in full battle by one blow of the lance, at the moment when he was crushing the last army of Monomachos. Hero or demigod capable of resuscitating the empire of Justinian, – vanishing in order to give way to a filthy imbecile! The bloodless head of that great man was nailed above the highest terrace of the Hippodrome.

All the same, it was not permitted to the sad sire to die in peace. In this way, at least, a semblance of justice seems to have been fulfilled, while waiting for what is not of this world. Five years later almost, the famous revolt of Tornikios broke out. Ah! it was not so pretty! However, never was an emperor so close to ruin as Monomachos was on that occasion. The dirty bastard was, this time again and more inexplicably, protected. There was a moment when the new pretender whose cretinism will never be surpassed, had merely to enter Constantinople with his army. An immense fear on the part of the people had opened the gates to him, and Monomachos could have been impaled that very same day. Stupidly, Tornikios waited to be called for, in triumph, like a Bourbon of the last century might have done. His eyes were gouged out, and no one knows what became of him.

Monomachos could breathe now and take care of his gout while contemplating, with a pacified soul, the last abominations of his reign. There had already been a formidable invasion of Russians easily dissipated by Greek fire, and a rosary of many thousands of their chopped-off hands were seen on the rampart of Constantinople. There was later, when one was beginning to forget about Maniakes and Tornikios, a prettier spectacle. That was the ruin of the great Erzurum, with its 800 churches, which the Empire had the duty to protect. The Turks killed 150,000 Christians there, burned the city, and led away more than 100,000 captives. More than 10,000 carts were needed to carry off the booty. To add insult to injury, the Sultan demanded of the Emperor, fifty years nearly before the first Crusade, the construction of a mosque in Constantinople, and he was obeyed...

How many other distractions! There was never a more amusing reign. When one was not massacring in Armenia, one was hacking the enemy to pieces on the Danube. No means to get bored. One

day, there was this poem of 15,000 barbarian horsemen swimming across the Bosporus. One can imagine
Monomachos' ravishment and dyspepsia on seeing it
from his palace. But the most interesting period of his
reign is assuredly the Keroularios[41] schism. Here, I
humbly ask Schlumberger to enlighten me on the following point:

After having said and repeated, on page 458,
that Michael Keroularios was a man "of high moral
valor," after having proclaimed "the known nobility
of his character," he reproaches him flat out for being
a total blackguard, accusing him, here and there, of
impiety, perfidy, deceit, assassination or instigation to
assassinate, finally and above all rebellion. So perfect
a contradiction can only be explained in one way.
Schlumberger lends his personal moral value to Keroularios and this latter, in return, regals him with the
honey of his schism.[42] So that is how it is with this patriarch just as with Luther, Calvin, or any other here-
siarch, whose moral hideousness is known by all edu-
cated men, but who have wrested from the Church
millions of souls only to hand them over to the Devil,
which effaces all their sins. Then, finally, that very
dignant successor to the dreadful Photius won.
Through him, generations of peoples since the ninth
century have been cut off from apostolic communion.
That is something alright.

---

[41]Keroularios: Michael I Keroularios (AD 1000-1059), Patriarch of
Constantinople.

[42]schism: the Great Schism of AD 1054. A schism between the
Eastern and Western churches of Constantinople and Rome.

A resolute basileus – such as Maniakes would have been, having, in the absence of pity, the intimate understanding of the imperial function which was totally lacking in Monomachos, – could have easily made that demoniac schism disappear, in the same way that Charles V would have had the power, just as he had the *duty*, to strike Luther, like lightning, going about it rather quickly. But both one and the other emperor would have needed to be those beneficent despots who could have saved the world and whom unfortunate men always hope for, without ever seeing them appear.

One can say that the miserable Constantine IX, called Monomachos, finished off his reign with the permission of Keroularios, whom his insolence, never chastised, had ended up making all-powerful, and who deigned to let him die while engaging in his overaged merrymaking. God help me from spending any more time pouring over such messy and sad and so distant already events of the Byzantine epic! The Macedonian dynasty, besides, is at its end; Zoe died in her piety, in her filth, and in her perfumes. The old Theodora reigns and dies in turn, about two years after Monomachos, having associated with the empire a stupid old man, Michael VI, the Stratiotikos, but commonly referred to as "the Old," who was made to take a tumble quietly, twelve months later, after having padded the stairs of the throne.

> *The last day of the month of August, 1057, Isaac, the first basileus of the glorious dynasty of the Komnenos,*

which was to govern the Empire to the extreme end of the following century, made his entry into the City protected by God, the queen of cities. A solemn thriambe[43] accompanied him to the Palace. On the following day, September 1, first day of the year in Byzantium, he was solemnly crowned by the patriarch before the ambon in the great church of Saint Sophia. He received the diadem and was proclaimed basileus and autocrator of the Romans. The imperial crown passed from the European portion to the Asiatic portion of the Empire. It was the triumph of the military element over the senatorial aristocracy and civil bureaucracy.

The glorious Macedonian dynasty, after nearly two centuries, gave way to that of the Komnenos, then the Angels, whom the French Crusaders were to overthrow one day.

One last word in order to ask forgiveness for

---

[43]*thriambe*: a triumph, e.g., triumphal hymns, music, celebration. "It appears that the Latin *triumphus* and the cry "*triumpe!*" share some relation to the Greek words *thriambos* and *thriambe*." See p. 44 of *Belief and Bloodshed: Religion and Violence across Time and Tradition*, James K. Wellman, Jr. etc. Rowman and Littlefield Publishers, Lantham, Maryland, 2007.

my impertinences.

Everyone belongs to the Institute. Only, Gustave Schlumberger is the author of *The Byzantine Epic*.

Other Books by the Publisher

Fanchette's Pretty Little Foot by Restif de La Bretonne

Je M'Accuse... by Léon Bloy

My Hospitals & My Prisons by Paul Verlaine

Salvation Through the Jews by Léon Bloy

Words of a Demolitions Contractor by Léon Bloy

Cellulely by Paul Verlaine

Ecclesiastical Laurels by Jacques Rochette de la Morlière

Flowers of Bitumen by Émile Goudeau

Songs for Her & Odes in Her Honor by Paul Verlaine

On Huysmans' Tomb by Léon Bloy

Ten Years a Bohemian by Émile Goudeau

The Soul of Napoleon by Léon Bloy

Blood of the Poor by Léon Bloy

Joan of Arc and Germany by Léon Bloy

A Platonic Love by Paul Alexis

The Revealer of the Globe: Christopher Columbus & His Future Beatification (Part One) by Léon Bloy

An Immodest Proposal by Dr. Helmut Schleppend

The Pornographer by Restif de La Bretonne

Style (Theory and History) by Ernest Hello

On the Threshold of the Apocalypse: 1913-1915 by Léon Bloy

She Who Weeps (Our Lady of La Salette) by Léon Bloy

The Sylph by Claude Prosper Jolyot de Crébillon (*fils*)

Voyage in France by a Frenchman by Paul Verlaine

Ourigan, Oregon by William Clark, Richard Robinson, and anonymous

Drowning by Yu Dafu

Cull of April by Francis Vielé-Griffin

The Misfortune of Monsieur Fraque by Paul Alexis

Fêtes Galantes & Songs Without Words by Paul Verlaine

Joys by Francis Vielé-Griffin

The Son of Louis XVI by Léon Bloy

Septentrion by Jean Raspail

The Resurrection of Villiers de l'Isle-Adam by Léon Bloy

Poems Saturnian by Paul Verlaine

The Biography of Léon Bloy: Memories of a Friend by René Martineau

Fredegund, France: A Book of Poetry by Richard Robinson

The Good Song by Paul Verlaine

Swans by Francis Vielé-Griffin